W9-CGS-154

HERO TALES

DAVE & NETA JACKSON

BETHANY HOUSE PUBLISHERS
MINNEAPOLIS, MINNESOTA 55438

Books by Dave and Neta Jackson

~ ~ ~ ~ ~ ~ ~ ~ ~ ~ ~ ~ ~ ~

Heroes in Black History

*Hero Tales: A Family Treasury of True Stories
From the Lives of Christian Heroes (Volumes I, II, and IV)*

Trailblazer Books

William & Catherine Booth ▪ *Kidnapped by River Rats*
John Bunyan ▪ *Traitor in the Tower*
Maude Cary ▪ *Risking the Forbidden Game*
Adoniram & Ann Judson ▪ *Imprisoned in the Golden City*
David Livingstone ▪ *Escape from the Slave Traders*
Martin Luther ▪ *Spy for the Night Riders*
Hudson Taylor ▪ *Shanghaied to China*

*Trailblazers: Featuring Harriet Tubman
and Other Christian Heroes*

*Trailblazers: Featuring Amy Carmichael
and Other Christian Heroes*

*Trailblazers: Featuring William Tyndale
and Other Christian Heroes*

*Trailblazers: Featuring David Livingstone
and Other Christian Heroes*

*Trailblazers: Featuring Martin Luther
and Other Christian Heroes*

Hero Tales: A Family Treasury of True Stories From the Lives of Christian Heroes
Copyright © 1996
Dave and Neta Jackson

Cover design by Peter Glöege.
Interior illustrations by Toni Auble

Scripture quotations, unless indicated, are from *The Holy Bible, New Century Version*, copyright ©
1987, 1988, 1991 by Word Publishing, Dallas, Texas 75039. Used by permission.

Scripture quotations identified NIV are taken from the HOLY BIBLE, NEW INTERNATIONAL
VERSION.® Copyright © 1973, 1978, 1984 by International Bible Society. Used by permission of
Zondervan Publishing House. All rights reserved. The "NIV" and "New International Version"
trademarks are registered in the United States Patent and Trademark Office by International Bible
Society. Use of either trademark requires the permission of International Bible Society.

Verses marked NKJV are from the New King James Version of the Bible.

All rights reserved. No part of this publication may be reproduced, stored in a retrieval system, or
transmitted in any form or by any means—electronic, mechanical, photocopying, recording, or
otherwise—without the prior written permission of the publisher. The only exception is brief
quotations in printed reviews.

Published by Bethany House Publishers
11400 Hampshire Avenue South
Bloomington, Minnesota 55438

Bethany House Publishers is a division of
Baker Publishing Group, Grand Rapids, Michigan.

Printed in the United States of America by RR Donnelley, Crawfordsville, IN.
March 2011, 8th printing

Volume I (Paperback):   ISBN 978-0-7642-0078-6
Volume II (Paperback):   ISBN 978-0-7642-0079-3
Volume III (Paperback): ISBN 978-0-7642-0080-9
Volume IV (Paperback):   ISBN 978-0-7642-0081-6

The Library of Congress has cataloged the hardcover edition as follows:

Jackson, Dave.
    Hero tales : a family treasury of true stories from the lives of Christian heroes / Dave and
Neta Jackson.
        p.   cm.
    Summary: Presents biographies of seventeen missionaries, evangelists, and other Christian heroes
who worked courageously to share the Gospel with others.

    1. Christian biography—Juvenile literature. 2. Missionaries—Biography—Juvenile literature.
[1. Christian biography. 2. Missionaries.] I. Jackson, Neta. II. Title.
BR1704.J33   1996
270'.092'2—dc20
[B]
                                                                        96-25230
                                                                            CIP
                                                                            AC

For Havah Noelle—

May you grow up knowing

true heroes and heroines.

CONTENTS ☙

CONTENTS

GLADYS AYLWARD

———————— ❦ ————————

The Small Woman

Born in London to a working-class family in 1902, Gladys Aylward had one wish: to go to China as a missionary. The China Inland Mission, however, did not think she was qualified. But the belief that God wanted her to go to China would not die. When Gladys heard that an elderly missionary in China wanted an assistant, she saved her money working as a maid and bought a one-way train ticket. She arrived in Yangcheng, China, in November 1932.

The missionary, Jennie Lawson, managed an inn for muleteers driving mule trains across the mountains. The inn not only offered people food and a place to sleep, but Bible stories told by the two missionaries.

But Jennie Lawson died a few months after Gladys's arrival, and Gladys had to continue the work alone.

In 1938, the Japanese bombed Yangcheng. Already Gladys had adopted several orphan children. Now there were many more orphans who came to live at her Inn of Eight Happinesses. But the

Japanese thought she was a spy, and it was no longer safe for her in Yangcheng. So in March 1940, Gladys escaped with a hundred children over the mountains to the next province. A month later, she arrived safely—without losing one child!

But Gladys was weak and ill. In 1942, an American friend helped her go back to England to see her family. While she was there, the Communists closed China to all foreigners.

In 1957, Gladys once again sailed for China, this time to Formosa. She started the Gladys Aylward Orphanage and soon had a hundred children. Here Gladys Aylward, the small woman who was not qualified to be a missionary, served God until her death in 1970.

CONFIDENCE
Not Good Enough

~~~~~~~~~~~~~~~~~~~~~~~~~~~~~~~

ladys Aylward sat uneasily in the principal's office. It was 1928, and she'd been at the China Inland Mission training school for three months. What was this meeting about?

"Gladys," the principal said gently, "your grades for the first quarter are . . . well, very poor. It would be a waste of time and money to continue."

"But," Gladys protested, "all my life I have felt that God wants me to be a missionary in China."

"Besides," the principal went on, "by the time you graduate, you will be almost thirty. That is too old to learn a hard language like Chinese."

Shoulders sagging, she rose to leave.

"But I can help you get a job as a housekeeper," he added helpfully.

A housekeeper! Gladys was frustrated. She was sure God wanted her to go to China. But she took the job housekeeping for two retired missionaries who encouraged her interest in missions. They got her a job as a Rescue Sister in South Wales patrolling the riverfront for runaway girls—girls who often fell into the hands of criminals. Only five feet tall, Gladys seemed out of place among the big, rough sailors along the docks. But she went out every day into the damp and cold, taking the frightened runaways to shelter until she could send them home again.

But a bad case of pneumonia sent her home to London to recover. While at church with her mother, she overheard someone talking about an elderly missionary in China named Jennie Lawson. Jennie wanted a young assistant to help her.

"Why," Gladys said to herself, "that's me!"

As soon as she was better, she got a job as a maid. She would save every penny to pay her way to China! Her employer was Sir Francis Younghusband, an author who had traveled all over China. He loaned her books about the country to read in her free time.

One day, Gladys took her savings to a travel agent. "What does it cost to travel to China?" she asked.

The travel agent smiled at the short woman in the thin coat. She was obviously poor. Maybe she was having fun pretending. "If you go by boat," he said, "it's ninety pounds."

Ninety pounds! Gladys only had a few pounds. "Is there a cheaper way?" she asked.

The ticket agent shrugged. "A *train* ticket is only forty-five pounds, but—"

"I'll take it!" Gladys beamed. "Write me a ticket, and I'll bring in money every Friday until it's paid for."

The agent shook his head. "You can't get to China by train right now. Russia and China are at war. The border is closed."

Gladys just smiled. "By the time I save enough money, the war will be over," she said confidently.

On October 15, 1932, Gladys hugged her mother and father

goodbye and settled into her train seat. Five thousand miles and four weeks later, she eased her aching body off a mule in front of a run-down inn in the mountain town of Yangcheng. White-haired Jennie Lawson scurried out to greet her.

Gladys Aylward, who was "not good enough" to be a missionary, had arrived in China!

Confidence is being sure that God will help you do His work, even when people think you can't do it.

FROM GOD'S WORD:

God began doing a good work in you, and I am sure he will continue it until it is finished when Jesus Christ comes again (Philippians 1:6).

LET'S TALK ABOUT IT:

1. Why do you think Gladys would not give up her dream of going to China even when the mission board told her she was not qualified?
2. What is the difference between confidence in yourself and confidence in God?
3. How can confidence in what God can do help you with a problem you're facing?

RESOURCEFULNESS
The Official Foot Inspector

ladys Aylward lay on the cot in her little sleeping room at the Inn of Eight Happinesses. She felt very alone. Jennie Lawson, the white-haired missionary who had wanted an assistant, had died of injuries from a fall less than a year after Gladys arrived.

"How am I going to pay the taxes for the inn?" Gladys worried. "The little bit of money we charge the mule drivers who stay here is only enough to buy food and coal. And the Chinese people still call me a 'foreign devil.' How will I ever get a chance to tell them about Jesus?" Then she scolded herself. "God brought me all the way to China. He won't leave me now."

Just then she heard an urgent tapping at her door. "Miss Gladys!" called Yang, the cook. "Come quickly. The Mandarin is here to see you!"

Gladys jumped up. *Oh no!* she thought. *The Mandarin must be angry because I haven't paid the taxes. Maybe he has come to take me to jail!* In spite of her nervousness, she hurried out into the courtyard, where the governor of the province was standing with several of his officials. He was a noble-looking man, with a long black pigtail down his back and a drooping moustache that hung below his jaw. His clothes were of fine silk, with wide sleeves that hid the hands clasped in front of him.

Gladys bent her head in a respectful bow. She noticed her own faded, patched blue coat and trousers.

But the Mandarin did not seem to notice. "Miss Aylward," he said respectfully, "I want you to become my official Foot Inspector."

Gladys was startled. "Y-your what?"

"The new Nationalist Government has outlawed the ancient practice of binding little girls' feet to keep them small. I need a Foot Inspector to go into the mountain villages to make sure the people are obeying the law."

"But . . . why me?" Gladys gasped.

"Because men are not allowed to see a woman's feet—and as a foreign woman, your feet have never been bound. I will give you a monthly salary, a mule to ride, and two soldiers to go with you. You will have my authority to make sure people obey the law."

Gladys's head was spinning. She had come to China to be a missionary, not a Foot Inspector! Was the Mandarin asking her or telling her? How would she have time to run the inn and tell people about Jesus if she accepted his offer? Unless . . .

"I will be honored to be your Foot Inspector," she said boldly, "on one condition. If I go to the villages, I must also have the freedom to talk to the people about Jesus."

The Mandarin shrugged. "If people want to listen to you talk about your religion, that is their business."

When the courtyard gate closed behind the Mandarin, Gladys leaned against it and laughed out loud. A short while ago, she had been worrying about money for taxes and how to be a missionary. God had just given her a way!

Resourcefulness is making use of all opportunities to do God's work.

FROM GOD'S WORD:

Look at the new thing I am going to do. It is already happening. Don't you see it? I will make a road in the desert and rivers in the dry land (Isaiah 43:19).

LET'S TALK ABOUT IT:

1. Why was Gladys Aylward feeling so discouraged about being a missionary in China?
2. When the Mandarin offered her a government job, how did Gladys plan to use it for God in a resourceful way?
3. What kinds of opportunities do you have that could be used in a resourceful way to do work for God?

COURAGE
The Man With the Axe

≈≈≈≈≈≈≈≈≈≈≈≈≈≈≈≈≈≈≈≈≈≈≈≈

Someone was pounding on the gate of the Inn of Eight Happinesses. "Gladys Aylward! You must come quickly!"

As Gladys followed the messenger, she could hear terrible screams coming from inside the local prison. It sounded like a riot. But why had the Mandarin sent for her? Confused, the small Englishwoman bowed respectfully to the Mandarin, who was standing with the governor of the prison.

"Thank goodness you have come!" said the governor, wringing his hands. "You must go in and stop the riot!"

Gladys was shocked. "*Me?* Why don't you send in your soldiers?"

"Impossible!" the man cried. "These prisoners are murderers and thieves! The soldiers would certainly be killed!"

"But," Gladys protested, "if *I* went in there, they would kill *me.*"

"Oh no," said the governor. "You tell our people that God lives inside you. If what you say is true, surely your God will protect you when you go inside the prison."

Gladys stared at the two men. Were they making fun of her? But they were serious. She realized that if she did not believe God could protect her, she could forget about being a missionary in China.

She swallowed hard. "All right," she said slowly. "Open the gate."

Gladys was so frightened her knees were shaking. Inside the prison courtyard, a horrible sight greeted her. Prisoners were chasing one another with knives and screaming like madmen. Dead and wounded prisoners were lying everywhere. And—running straight toward her was a huge man holding an axe over his head!

Gladys was so terrified she couldn't move. But when the man was only a few feet away, he suddenly stopped. One by one, the other prisoners stopped yelling and running and just looked at her. Who was this short little woman? What was she doing here?

Suddenly, Gladys got mad. The man with the axe was just a big bully. "Give me that axe!" she demanded, holding out her hand.

Without a word, the man handed her the axe.

Gladys looked at the prisoners. They were dressed in dirty rags. They were so thin their ribs showed. They looked cold and miserable. Suddenly, instead of being afraid of them, she felt sorry for them. "I have been sent by the governor of the prison to find out why you are fighting."

At first, no one spoke. Then a young prisoner came forward. "My name is Feng," he said. "We don't know why we are fighting . . . but we are hungry and have nothing to do day after day."

Gladys frowned. These men had been locked up like animals, without enough food and no work to keep them busy. "If you will promise to stop fighting, and will bury the dead and take care of those who are wounded, I will speak to the governor for you," she said.

The prisoners agreed. As Gladys stepped outside the prison, the city officials bowed to her with respect. She told the governor of the prison that the men needed to have work to do so they could earn money, buy food, and have self-respect—and she, Gladys Aylward, was going to come back to visit the prison every day to make sure it happened!

Courage is knowing God's power can help you do something hard even when you feel scared.

FROM GOD'S WORD:

For God has not given us a spirit of fear, but of power and of love and of a sound mind (2 Timothy 1:7, NKJV).

LET'S TALK ABOUT IT:

1. Why did Gladys agree to go inside a prison full of dangerous prisoners?
2. Can you be scared and have courage at the same time? Why or why not?
3. What is the difference between doing something foolish just to "prove" that you're not scared, and doing something that takes courage even though you're afraid?

WILLIAM & CATHERINE BOOTH

Founders of the Salvation Army

Both William Booth and his wife, Catherine (Mumford) Booth, were born in England in 1829. It was while they were young people that they became concerned about the harm alcohol did to families. In fact, they first met at a friend's house where William quoted a poem about the dangers of alcohol. They were later married in 1855.

Both William and Catherine were especially interested in reaching out to poor people. To help them and show them God's love, they opened the East London Christian Mission in 1865. Soon William began calling it the "Salvation Army." He and Catherine believed that to save people from evil and teach them about Jesus Christ, Christians needed to organize like an army—the Lord's army—going into spiritual battle. Their newspaper was *The War Cry*, their leaders were "officers," Christians were "captives," and people called William "General." Outreaches into new cities or countries became known as "invasions."

The street-corner preaching of the Salvation Army was so useful in bringing people to Christ and encouraging them to stop drinking that business began to drop off at the gin shops. In response, the tavern owners encouraged troublemakers to attack the Salvationists. In 1882 alone, 669 Salvationists were attacked and sixty of the Army's buildings were wrecked by mobs.

By 1872, the Salvation Army had opened five lunch rooms where—day or night—the poor could buy a cup of soup for a quarter of a penny or a complete meal for six cents. Thousands of meals were given away free.

Catherine died in 1890 at the age of sixty-one. William Booth continued the ministry of the Salvation Army. Before he died on August 20, 1912, at the age of eighty-three, he traveled around the world and preached sixty thousand sermons.

CREATIVITY
The General's Boxer

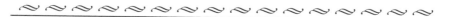

eter Monk boxed for money while other men bet on who would win. The fights usually took place on London's east side behind a pub called The Blind Beggar.

One day, Monk met a well-dressed minister on the sidewalk near the pub. He usually paid no attention to ministers, but this man caught his notice when he said, "I'm looking for work."

Surprised, the burly boxer reached into his pocket to offer him some money. But the gentleman waved him off and pointed toward a group of men standing outside the pub. "Look at those men," said William Booth, for he was the minister who had stopped the boxer. "Look at them—forgotten by God and man. Why should I be looking for work? There's my work, looking for me."

Monk was puzzled by these strange comments, but he agreed with one thing. "You are right, sir. Those men *are* forgotten by God and man, and if you can do anything for them, it would be a great work."

"Well, I'll be preaching tomorrow evening in that tent on the corner. Come and bring a few of the boys with you."

Without knowing why, Monk said yes.

For the next day's fight, Monk faced a tough Irishman like himself, only larger. It was a long and hard fight before Monk finally dropped his opponent with a series of blows to the body and a final punch to the jaw. Monk's fans cheered and collected their gambling winnings, but Monk felt no joy as he picked up his prize money.

Then he remembered the minister and headed off to the tent, his face still swollen and blood-streaked.

When he arrived, some of the neighborhood troublemakers were yelling insults so loudly that no one could hear what the preacher was saying. Monk watched for a moment. Then, remembering that William Booth had said these were forgotten men who needed God, Monk walked to the front and climbed up onto the platform.

He took off his jacket, folded his arms across his sweat-stained shirt, and stared at the crowd. A hush fell over the people as they recognized him. Even the troublemakers respected him.

Booth used the silence to preach a powerful sermon. Afterward he approached the fighter and thanked him. Then he said, "You're not happy, Peter Monk."

"How do you know?"

"You're living for the devil, and you'll die like a dog."

"Ha! Who made you a prophet?"

"Well, my Father in heaven. But tell me, am I right? You're not happy, are you?"

Monk came back to hear more of what this bold preacher had to say. Within a few days, he had given his life to the Lord Jesus Christ. He then volunteered to join William Booth to help keep troublemakers under control at his meetings and do whatever else might help reach the men of the streets.

Creativity means coming up with new ways to reach people and do God's work.

FROM GOD'S WORD:

To those who are weak, I became weak so I could win the weak. I have become all things to all people so I could save some of them in any way possible (1 Corinthians 9:22).

LET'S TALK ABOUT IT:

1. Why do you think William Booth chose a boxer to speak to in order to reach the men outside the pub?
2. Why did Booth say, "I'm looking for work"?
3. What is a creative way you have seen someone use to share the Good News with people?

BOLDNESS

"Come Hear a Woman Preach!"

~~~~~~~~~~~~~~~~~~~~~~~~~~~

hat's the matter, my dear?" asked William Booth. He had just finished his morning sermon in a local church when his wife, Catherine, rose from her seat and walked forward to the pulpit.

"I want to say a word," Catherine said to him in a hushed voice.

Surprised, William did not know what to do. It was so unusual for a woman to speak to a group of people that many thought it was wrong. But William trusted his wife. If she had something she needed to say, then he would let her.

"My dear wife wishes to speak," he announced.

Catherine stepped up onto the platform and began to preach. Before she finished, the people were crying and coming forward to repent and ask forgiveness for their sins. The congregation had never heard a woman speak so powerfully.

That afternoon, as she tried to explain what had happened, all she could say was, "I felt the Holy Spirit . . . all the way down to my hands and feet. It seemed as if a voice said, 'If you will go and testify, you know I will bless you as well as those who hear you.'"

That evening, the chapel was packed with more people who wanted to hear a woman preach.

Not long after this, William became ill, and Catherine took over his speaking schedule. Soon people were announcing her meetings as if she were a circus act: "Come hear a woman preach!" The curious came, but God used their curiosity to change their lives.

Catherine's boldness truly made a difference when, later, she spoke to over two hundred poor women from London's streets. Many of them gave their lives to Jesus. Some of them volunteered to start Rescue Homes where homeless girls and women could go for protection and to start a new life. One home took in eight hundred girls in three years.

Until the Salvation Army reached out to them, these street people had mostly been forgotten by the rest of the church. But Catherine cared, and her example earned her the nickname of "The Army Mother."

When she was sixty years old and dying of cancer, Catherine was still preaching boldly. To her last audience, she said, "Be encouraged by what you have heard of what God has done. . . . Make up your mind as the General did when he was eighteen, that he would spend every bit of his strength, every nerve of his body, and all he had in preaching salvation."

Boldness may require doing the unusual.

FROM GOD'S WORD:

And now, Lord, listen to their threats. Lord, help us, your servants, to speak your word without fear (Acts 4:29).

LET'S TALK ABOUT IT:

1. Why did Catherine Booth feel she needed to say something after William had preached?
2. How did Catherine's boldness help homeless women in London?
3. Describe a place where boldness is needed today.

DISCIPLINE
Training for a
Young Soldier

~~~~~~~~~~~~~~~~~~~~~~~~~~~~~~~~~~

Go home!" shouted a drunk as he leaned on the bar and shook his fist at William Booth. "And take that skinny kid with you."

Some of the other people in the pub hooted and jeered . . . but not all. A few were leaning close to the dim lamps to read the gospel tracts that William and his thirteen-year-old son, Bramwell, had handed out.

"The Lord loves you and can rescue you from your wickedness," yelled William over the hubbub. "Come to the meeting at the New East London Theater tomorrow night, and He will save you."

"You can have your religion," roared one drinker. Then he raised his glass and added, "*This* is our religion!"

As they left the pub, Booth turned to his son and said, "These are the people I want you to live and work with, Bramwell. The poor have nothing but these terrible gin shops and their drink. But we can give them the Good News about Jesus Christ. These are our people. We must tell them that Jesus can save them from the devil."

The slums of East London were a sad place to be at this time. It was said that every fifth house was a "gin shop" with special steps to help even the tiniest children reach the counter. By five years of age, many children were alcoholics. Some even died.

But the street-corner preaching of the Salvation Army worked. In fact, so many people came to know Christ and stopped drinking and gambling that business began to slow at the gin shops. The owners, who had been getting rich by selling alcohol to these poor people, were not happy and did everything they could to stop the street-corner preachers. But God would not let them stop the work of the Salvation Army.

This was a rough place for young Bramwell Booth to learn to tell others about Christ. But it made him strong. When he was sixteen, Bramwell took over running the Food-for-the-Million shops that helped to feed poor people. There were five canteens, open twenty-four hours a day, that sold a cup of soup for a quarter of a penny and a whole meal for six cents. Bramwell had learned his lessons well, and promised to give his life to bringing the Good News about Jesus Christ to the poor.

When he grew up, Bramwell became the chief of staff for the Salvation Army. It was his job to plan and direct the missionary work of the Salvation Army in countries all over the world.

When William Booth was dying, the old general called his son to him. "Bramwell," the weak old man said, "the promises of God are sure." He waved his shaky finger in the air. "If you only believe."

Later, his last words were, "I am leaving you a bonnie handful, Bramwell." He was talking about the big job of leading the Salvation Army. General William Booth had chosen his son to become the Salvation Army's second general.

Discipline means training to become stronger, not just correction when you do something wrong.

FROM GOD'S WORD:

So hold on through your sufferings, because they are like a father's discipline. God is treating you as children. All children are disciplined by their fathers (Hebrews 12:7).

LET'S TALK ABOUT IT:

1. Why did William Booth take his son into the gin shops?
2. What did Bramwell learn from the way his father treated the poor?
3. Describe some training you have had that was hard but made you stronger.

AMY CARMICHAEL

Dohnavur Fellowship, India

Amy Carmichael was born on December 16, 1867, in Northern Ireland, the daughter of a respected mill owner. When Amy was only seventeen years old, she began having Sunday classes for the "shawlies"—the girls who worked in the mills and wore shawls. These meetings grew so quickly that Amy decided they needed a building in which to hold them. Her faith and vision were catching, and soon the mill girls were meeting in a new hall named "The Welcome" for Bible study, music practice, night school, sewing club, mothers' meeting, and a monthly gospel meeting open to everyone.

In 1892, when she was twenty-four years old, Amy heard God's call for her to take the Good News to people in foreign countries. Recommended by leaders of the Keswick Convention, she was accepted by the Church of England Zenana Missionary Society and sent to India in October 1895. Little did anyone know she would never return home again.

Amy threw herself into studying Tamil, the language of

southern India, and in time gathered together a group of Christian Indian women who called themselves the Starry Cluster. These women went from village to village preaching the Gospel. As they traveled, Amy Carmichael became aware of the "temple children," young girls who were "married to the gods" in the Hindu temples, a practice that included prostitution. To provide a home for these girls, Amy established Dohnavur (*doh-nah-voor*) Fellowship. Soon Amy Carmichael became *Amma* (mother) to dozens of little girls. Later the ministry expanded to include little boys.

In October 1931, at the age of sixty-four, Amy fell into a pit, breaking her leg. She never fully recovered and spent the next twenty years confined to her room. She wrote thirteen books after her accident, in addition to updating her earlier books. These books capture many stories of the lives of boys and girls, men and women, who came to know God through the work of Dohnavur Fellowship.

Amy Carmichael died on January 18, 1951, but her spirit lives on in the work of Dohnavur Fellowship, still going strong in south India today.

SACRIFICE
The Best Jewels of All

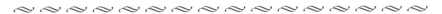

When Amy Carmichael first came to India as a missionary, she decided to wear the Indian *sari* and fit in to Indian culture as best she could. Although she didn't wear jewelry, Amy thought the gold and silver necklaces, bangles, rings, anklets, and earrings the Indian women wore were very pretty.

Even the members of the Starry Cluster—the group of Christian Indian women who went with Amy from village to village sharing the Good News about Jesus—were decked out head to toe in jewels. But Amy soon learned that, in India, a woman's jewels were a source of pride. They showed how rich her family was, how important her husband was, or what caste or social group she belonged to. Amy was worried—it did not seem good for Christians to care about these things. Still, she hesitated to say anything. She did not like how some missionaries made the Indian Christians adopt English-looking clothes and ways of doing things.

"Lord," she prayed, "if you want the women to give up their

jewels, have the women themselves ask whether they should, not me."

One day Ponnamal, a member of the Starry Cluster, heard a child say, "When I grow up, I want to join the Starry Cluster so I can wear jewels like Ponnamal does." This bothered the sincere Indian woman. That was not a good reason to join the Cluster!

Ponnamal prayed and asked God what she should do. She knew that an Indian woman with no jewels would be laughed at. But then God seemed to say to her, "You will be a crown of glory in the hand of the Lord." Ponnamal realized that *she* was like a jewel to God, even if she wore no jewelry at all.

Ponnamal took off all her jewels. One by one, the other women in the Starry Cluster also took off their jewels. Sure enough, many people laughed at them. These Christians were very strange! But some women and girls noticed how these Christians loved and served one another, just like they were sisters, regardless of wealth or caste. Many more came to join the group—and later to be workers at Dohnavur Fellowship. How could people tell they were a part of this special group? None of the women wore any jewels. But many took new names like "Jewel of Victory" or "Jewel of Praise."

Many years later, a watchman for a robber band told Amy, "If those hundreds of girls wore jewels according to Indian custom, not all the money in the world could hire a watchman to guard them." With a thankful heart, Amy realized that God had used the women's sacrifice of giving up their jewels to protect them from harm and danger.

*Sacrifice includes being willing to give up
something for God.*

FROM GOD'S WORD:

So brothers and sisters, since God has shown us
great mercy, I beg you to offer your lives as a living
sacrifice to him. Your offering must be only for God
and pleasing to him, which is the spiritual way for
you to worship (Romans 12:1).

LET'S TALK ABOUT IT:

1. Why did Ponnamal decide to take off her jewels?
2. How did this affect the way the Christian Indian
   women thought about themselves? How did it
   affect the way other women thought about them?
3. How can we offer ourselves as "living sacrifices"
   to God in our country? Be as detailed as possible.

COMPASSION
"The Child-Catching
Missie Ammal"

s Amy Carmichael and the Starry Cluster went from village to village preaching the Gospel, she noticed small girls who seemed to live in the Hindu temples. They were beautifully dressed and very graceful. "Who are those children?" she asked.

"Those are the temple children," Ponnamal replied sadly. "They are married to the gods."

Amy was shocked. How could anyone give or sell their child to the temple? Gradually she learned why. If parents were not able to arrange a good marriage (which, in India, was done at an early age), their child was "married to the gods" to avoid disgrace. Or a widow might sell her child to the temple to get much-needed money. Or maybe it was to fulfill a religious vow or promise. Whatever the reason, Amy knew it was a terrible life for a child.

She decided to do something about it. Sometimes she tried to get the children away from the temples. But the temple children were watched night and day.

"Watch out," the children were told, "or you will be captured by that child-catching Missie Ammal." (*Ammal* means "mother" in Tamil.)

On March 6, 1901, Amy and the Starry Cluster returned late at night to their village of Pannaivilai after many months on the road. The next morning as Amy relaxed on the porch sipping her tea, a neighbor woman appeared with a young girl she had found the night before.

The child crawled right into Amy's lap. "Are you the child-catching Missie Ammal?" the little girl asked. "My name is Preena, and I want to stay with you—always!"

Gradually Preena told her story. Her mother had "married her to the gods," but she was always scared. Once she ran away and went home to her mother. But her mother took her right back to the temple, and her hands had been branded with a hot iron for running away. She was watched closely.

Still seven-year-old Preena wanted to run away. How she slipped past the temple guards on March 6, no one knows. (*An angel must have led her out of her prison*, Amy thought, *just like the apostle Peter*.) If Preena had escaped a few days earlier, Amy would not have been home. And if the neighbor had found the girl earlier in the day, she would have taken her back to the temple already. Only God could have planned it so well.

Now Amy was sure God had sent Preena to her to take care of. *But*, the missionary thought, *how can I take care of a small girl while traveling from village to village preaching about Jesus Christ?*

God soon gave her an answer. When more temple children came to her for protection, Amy realized she and the Starry Cluster needed to quit traveling and make a home for them. She called the home Dohnavur Fellowship.

An ancient Indian proverb says, "Children tie the feet of the mother"—meaning a mother is not free to come and go as she pleases. Her duty is first of all to her children. Amy let her feet be "tied" because she had compassion on the temple children. She didn't just feel sorry for them. She let her compassion for them change her life.

*Compassion is sympathy for another person
that goes beyond just feeling sorry and
makes you take action.*

FROM GOD'S WORD:
"This is what the LORD All-Powerful says: 'Do what is right and true. Be kind and merciful to each other'" (Zechariah 7:9).

LET'S TALK ABOUT IT:
1. Why did Amy feel compassion for the temple children?
2. What did her compassion do for the temple children? What changes did it make in Amy's life?
3. Is there someone in your neighborhood or school you feel sorry for? How would being "kind and merciful" help that person? How would it change your life?

SERVANTHOOD
Messy Work for God

he bell on the gate of Dohnavur Fellowship rang and rang. When Amy Carmichael opened the gate, a local pastor was standing there holding a baby.

"She's only thirteen days old," he said. "I rescued her from a Hindu temple. Will you take her, Amma?"

"Ohhh," ten-year-old Preena said when she saw the small, puckered face. "Can I name her?" Preena was the first temple child who came to live with Amy. When Amy smiled and nodded, Preena said, "Let's call her *Amethyst*—it's one of the jewels in the Holy City."

When another baby was brought to Dohnavur, Preena named her Sapphire.

By 1904, there were seventeen children living at Dohnavur Fellowship—six had been rescued from the Hindu temples. But these little "jewels" were a lot of work, especially the babies. Feeding, burping, changing diapers, rocking, hushing . . . and then it had to be done all over again. Sometimes when Amy was rocking a crying baby, she remembered the thrill of traveling from village to village telling people about Jesus. Had she done the right thing to give up that important work just to take care of babies?

Then Amy reread the Bible story about when Jesus kneeled down and washed the feet of His disciples. It was dirty work, the work of a servant. Then Jesus told His disciples to follow His example.

"All right, I will. I'm God's servant," Amy agreed. "And He *did* give me these little ones to care for."

But for the women of the Starry Cluster who helped Amy, it was not so easy. In India, everything was decided by the *caste* or social group you belonged to: what kind of work you did, who you could marry, who your friends were. There was a ruling caste, a metal-workers caste, a farmers caste, a medical caste, a cart-makers caste, a street-sweepers caste, on and on. Even servants belonged to different castes. The person who served dinner wouldn't wash the pots and pans!

One day, a new Christian came to Dohnavur Fellowship and wanted to help with the babies. But when Amy asked her to wash the nursery floor, she refused. "I can't! It's against my caste! It would be too humiliating," she protested.

Amy took the bucket of soapy water and got down on her knees. "Housework," she said gently, "like any other job, is God's work. Whatever we do becomes a good and holy task if we do it for God."

The new helper was ashamed to see the Irish missionary on her knees cheerfully scrubbing the nursery floor after she had refused to do it.

But Ponnamal, the wise Indian woman who had been with Amy since the beginning, smiled knowingly. "Amma never asks us to do anything she doesn't do herself."

Servanthood is doing any kind of work
to please Jesus.

FROM GOD'S WORD:

"If I, your Lord and Teacher, have washed your feet, you also should wash each other's feet. I did this as an example so that you should do as I have done for you" (John 13:14–15).

LET'S TALK ABOUT IT:

1. What do you think: Was giving up traveling and preaching the Gospel in order to take care of children a good choice for Amy Carmichael? Why or why not?
2. Why do you think Amy washed the floor, instead of just telling the new helper to do it?
3. What can you do today to follow Jesus' example of servanthood?

ADONIRAM &
ANN JUDSON

America's First Foreign
Missionaries

Adoniram Judson and Ann Hassletine were married on February 5, 1812, in Bradford, Massachusetts. Fourteen days later, the newlyweds set sail for India. They were going to be a part of foreign missions!

The British East India Company, however, didn't want any missionaries to get in the way of their money-making and forced them to leave the country. But where could they go? God had called them to preach the Gospel to people who had never heard it! In faith, they boarded a ship heading for *Burma*—a country hostile to foreigners, ruled by a king who had the power to decide who lived and died. In Burma, it was against the law to worship any other god than Buddha. But when they landed in Rangoon, Burma, the Judsons knew *this* was where God wanted them to be.

Their first task was to learn the hard language. Bit by bit, Adoniram worked on an English-Burmese dictionary and translated the books of the Bible. After six years, they baptized their first Christian convert. When the little church in Rangoon grew to eighteen, the Judsons sailed up the Irrawaddy River to begin a mission in Ava, the royal city.

In 1824, war broke out between England and Burma, and the Burmese became suspicious of all foreigners, thinking they were English spies. Adoniram was thrown into the Death Prison. After a year and a half of torture and misery, he was released to help translate the peace treaty between Burma and England.

By then, tropical fevers and stress had broken Ann's health. She died two years later; two-year-old Marie died six months later. (They had already lost a baby.) Adoniram struggled with grief and doubt for several years, but in time finished his translation of the entire Bible. He died in 1850 at the age of sixty-two and was buried at sea.

TRUTHFULNESS
The Talking Place

~~~~~~~~~~~~~~~~~~~~~~~~~~~~~~~~~

hen Adoniram and Ann Judson arrived in Burma in 1813, the first thing they had to do was learn the language. A former Buddhist monk named Maung Shwa-gnong agreed to be their teacher.

However, after the Judsons had been in Burma almost six years, not one Burmese had become a Christian.

"People are polite, but no one wants to talk about Jesus," Adoniram said.

"You have translated two tracts and the book of Matthew," Ann said. "At least now people can read the Good News in their own language."

"Yes, that's true," Adoniram agreed. "But we have to find a way to actually talk to people."

"If you want to talk about religion," Maung Shwa-gnong said, "you have to build a *zayat*." The American missionaries had seen these platforms on stilts along Pagoda Way—the street that led to the Great Golden Pagoda. "The *zayats* are where men gather to talk about philosophy and religion," the language teacher added.

Excited, Adoniram built a *zayat* and sat under the thatch roof waiting to talk about Jesus. Sure enough, first one man, then another, came and sat in the *zayat*. This was the way people in Burmese culture talked about religion.

"What does your religion say about the mind?" a man named Maung Nau asked, hoping for a good debate.

Adoniram said simply, "Our Bible says, 'Brothers and sisters, think about the things that are good and worthy of praise.'" Then Adoniram added, "How we think is how we act."

"What?" said Maung Nau. "That's impossible. We cannot live without telling lies!"

Adoniram was surprised. "What do you mean?"

"The king's word in Burma is law. If he doesn't like what you say, he can cut off your head—just like that. So you say whatever you think the king—or the mayor—wants to hear. Nobody trusts anyone else. It's the only way to stay alive!"

Adoniram realized that the way the Burmese people thought made it hard to understand Bible truths. "But our religion is based on truth," he said. "God's Son said, 'I am the Truth.' People who believe in Jesus must also do and say what is true."

The men went away shaking their heads. These strange Christian ideas could be dangerous!

Still, Adoniram, Maung Nau, and a few other men continued to talk in the *zayat*. Maung Shwa-gnong also listened. Then one day Maung Nau said, "I have decided to become a Jesus follower. I want to be baptized."

This was what Adoniram had been praying for! But he hesitated. He knew Maung Nau was risking his life by becoming a Christian.

Then Maung Nau said, "I am tired of cheating and lying. I want to follow the true God."

Adoniram and Ann rejoiced! They were so excited. And

within a few years, the little church in Rangoon had eighteen Burmese Christians—including Maung Shwa-gnong, the language teacher.

Truthfulness helps point people to Jesus, who is "the Truth, the Way, and the Life."

FROM GOD'S WORD:
But we have turned away from secret and shameful ways. We use no trickery, and we do not change the teaching of God. We teach the truth plainly, showing everyone who we are. Then they can know in their hearts what kind of people we are in God's sight (2 Corinthians 4:2).

LET'S TALK ABOUT IT:
1. Why was it important to actually talk to the Burmese people about Jesus?
2. Do you agree that "how we think is how we act"? Why or why not?
3. Christians say we believe in the one, true God. Why is it important for us to tell the truth and be honest with others?

PERSEVERANCE
The Book in the Pillow

〜〜〜〜〜〜〜〜〜〜〜〜〜〜〜〜〜〜〜〜

A doniram!" Ann Judson called to her husband. "Koo-chill says our supper is ready."

Wearily, Adoniram Judson put away the manuscript he'd been working on. The Judsons had been in Burma for thirteen years. The language was hard and translating the Bible was slow work. Burma and England were at war, so the American missionaries worked quietly in their bamboo home on stilts. It was too dangerous to do mission work in public.

Adoniram and Ann and their two Burmese foster daughters started to eat Koo-chill's tasty fish soup. Suddenly the door burst open and several men rushed inside. "Mr. Judson? You are under arrest!" said the city magistrate sternly. "Tie him up!"

"What is the charge?" gasped Adoniram as two men roughly tied his arms behind his back.

"The English are paying you. You are spies!" accused the magistrate.

"No, no!" cried Ann. Her frightened girls hid behind Koo-chill the cook. "Our English friends simply cashed our mission checks from America."

But in spite of Ann's pleas, Adoniram was dragged away and thrown into the dreaded Death Prison, along with several English prisoners also thought to be spies.

When Ann finally got permission to visit her husband two days later, it was hard to be brave. At night, the prisoners' feet were tied to a pole that was lifted into the air so that only their shoulders touched the ground.

"Where is my manuscript?" Adoniram asked hoarsely.

"I buried it beneath the house," Ann whispered back.

"That is the first place they will look!"

Ann looked thoughtful. "Don't worry. I have a plan."

The next time Ann came to see her husband, she brought a pillow—a hard, lumpy pillow that no other prisoner would want to steal. A secret smile passed between them.

For eleven months, Ann visited her husband in the Death Prison as often as she could. She brought baby Maria, born while her daddy was in prison, to see him. But one day when Ann arrived at the prison, it was empty! No one knew where the prisoners had been taken.

As Adoniram was forced to march in chains to a new prison, he felt sick at heart. The guards had refused to let him take the precious pillow. They had thrown it into the garbage. Thirteen years of work translating the Bible—in the trash!

Finally, the king released Adoniram to help translate a peace treaty between England and Burma. Then he was allowed to go back to his family. Adoniram was happy to be home with his wife and child—but he was discouraged.

"Everything is lost," he moaned. "We will have to start all over again."

Ann just smiled. Gently, she placed a hard, lumpy pillow in Adoniram's hands. His mouth fell open. The manuscript was safe inside! A Burmese Christian had discovered the pillow on the garbage heap and brought it safely home.

Now the Burmese people could have the Word of God in their own language.

Perseverance is sticking to the task God has given you, even when it means suffering.

FROM GOD'S WORD:
We also rejoice in our sufferings, because we know that suffering produces perseverance; perseverance, character; and character, hope (Romans 5:3–4, NIV).

LET'S TALK ABOUT IT:
1. Why was Adoniram's work of translating the Bible into the Burmese language so important?
2. How do you think Adoniram felt when he was locked in prison for months and months where he couldn't do any "mission" work? What was God doing during this time?
3. Is there something you know God wants you to do, but you get discouraged and feel like giving up? Talk about what helps you *persevere* (keep going) during those times.

FORGIVENESS
The Peace Treaty Feast

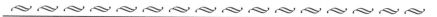

he war between Burma and England was over! Adoniram and Ann Judson were weak from the hard times during the past two years. Exhausted, they were on their way down the Irrawaddy River back to Rangoon.

"I wonder if the little church of eighteen Christians survived the war?" Adoniram said.

Partway down the river, the Burmese rowers pulled ashore. They had arrived at the British army camp. The army was getting ready to leave Burma. Sir Archibald Campbell met the two American missionaries as they stepped off the rowboat.

"Welcome!" the general cried. "I am having a special dinner for the Burmese officials who signed the peace treaty. You will be my honored guests!"

Even though the Judsons had not taken sides in the war between Burma and England, it felt good to be treated so royally. Instead of a dirty prison, they were given a large, comfortable tent. Instead of gruff officials ignoring them, the British officers happily tried to grant their every wish. The soldiers thought it was an honor to have a heroic woman like Ann Judson visiting their camp. They had heard stories of how she had faithfully visited her husband in prison, and how she had bravely worked for his freedom.

On the day of the dinner, the band played. Flags were flying. Ann's eyes sparkled. What a festive party! But when she walked in on the arm of the British general, one of the Burmese officials suddenly looked like he wished the ground would open and swallow him.

This was the frail lady he had once kept waiting for hours! She had come to beg him to take off the five leg-irons which chained her sick husband in prison. "No," he had shrugged. When she had turned to leave, he said, "Wait. Give me your silk parasol. My wife thinks it is pretty."

"Please, no! I need it to keep the hot sun off my head," Ann had said. "I am not well—I might faint on the way home."

But the official had just laughed and stole it anyway.

Now here she was—the honored guest of the British general who had just won the war! Surely she would seek revenge. After all, that's what *he* would do if someone had treated him so badly.

To his surprise, Ann Judson came over to him. "Don't be afraid," she said kindly. "I do not hold a grudge against you. Please, relax and enjoy this special dinner."

But the man could not relax. All through the dinner he sweated and shook, wondering when she would tell the British soldiers to drag him out and shoot him. But nothing happened. He left the dinner shaking his head. "I don't understand these Christians," he muttered. "They forgive their enemies!"

Forgiveness means not taking revenge on people who have treated you badly.

FROM GOD'S WORD:

"But I say to you who are listening, love your enemies. Do good to those who hate you, bless those who curse you, pray for those who are cruel to you" (Luke 6:27–28).

LET'S TALK ABOUT IT:

1. Why did the Burmese official feel so scared when he saw Ann Judson at the peace treaty dinner?
2. Why do you think Ann Judson was able to forgive this man?
3. Do you know someone who has treated you unkindly? Talk about it with your family. What would happen if you treated this person kindly? Ask God to give you the courage to forgive this person.

DAVID LIVINGSTONE

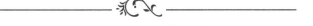

Explorer Missionary
to Africa

David Livingstone was born on March 19, 1813, on an island off the coast of Scotland. He grew up in a Christian home where his father was a tea merchant.

After studying medicine at Glasgow University in 1840, Livingstone went to South Africa with the London Missionary Society. What he saw there troubled him. The mission stations seemed more interested in creating comfortable British outposts than in reaching the people of Africa. Some of the missionaries were even racist. They thought that the Africans were best suited for being servants or field hands. But Livingstone believed that African Christians—once trained—made better missionaries to their own people than the English did.

Livingstone quickly mastered several African languages and learned the ways of the people. Shortly after he married Mary Moffat in 1844, the Livingstones set out to build a new mission station on the frontier. From there he planned to travel deep into

Africa, where the people had never heard the Gospel before.

But before long, he realized that he wasn't a preacher or an evangelist. God wanted him to explore the country and open new areas so other missionaries could follow. This he did in three trips.

Livingstone died on April 30, 1873. Chuma and Susi, two of his faithful African friends, carefully wrapped and embalmed his body and carried it to the coast. Chuma then went with the body to England, where Livingstone was buried with great honor. Chuma met with the queen and told others in England about the travels and expeditions of David Livingstone.

THANKFULNESS
Attacked by a Lion

hen David Livingstone first arrived in South Africa, most missionaries worked along the coast. "There are too many missionaries here!" he said. "I want to go where people have never heard the Good News before."

The people in charge of the mission thought young Livingstone had too many big ideas. One of these ideas was to train African Christians to be missionaries.

"When white men preach," Livingstone argued, "Africans just think we are talking about our odd European ways and customs. But when their own people tell them about Jesus, they see the truth

But the mission board didn't want to support African teachers, so David Livingstone raised some money himself. When he finally got permission to begin a mission at Mabotsa, two hundred miles into the interior of Africa, he took along an African teacher named Mebalwe.

For three months, Livingstone and his friends worked to build the new mission station. But one day, he heard that lions were eating cattle in a nearby village.

"Ordinary lions don't attack during the day," the villagers said. "These must be devil lions!" They were afraid to fight them.

"Don't be afraid," said Livingstone, interrupting the work on the new station. "Mebalwe, come with me. If we shoot one, that'll scare the others off."

Sure enough, soon after they arrived, a lion boldly broke into one of the cattle pens. Livingstone raised his gun and fired both barrels. The lion jerked back and roared. Quickly, Livingstone reloaded.

Mebalwe yelled a warning. Livingstone looked up just as the lion sprang. It caught Livingstone's shoulder in its huge jaws, crushing the bone. Both man and animal rolled in the dust.

When the lion came to its feet, it shook Livingstone like a rag doll. Livingstone thought, *I wonder what part of me he will eat first?*

Mebalwe raised his gun, but it misfired. The lion immediately dropped Livingstone and attacked the African teacher, burying his teeth in Mebalwe's leg. When another man tried to spear the lion, it turned and charged him—and then suddenly fell dead as Livingstone's two bullets finally did their job.

Sure enough, the other lions ran off and didn't come back. But Livingstone and Mebalwe were badly injured. It was a hard time for the brand-new mission. But Livingstone wrote to his father in Scotland, praising and thanking God for saving him from great danger.

Even though David Livingstone couldn't work on the building project because of his injuries, he *was* able to watch over the work until it was finished. But he needed more rest. He left Mebalwe at the new mission and traveled back to headquarters, where a young woman named Mary Moffat nursed him back to health. She was the daughter of Robert Moffat, mission director and well-known Bible translator. She admired this rugged young missionary who was not afraid to go where no white person had gone before. And he was impressed by her gentle, steady character. Livingstone asked her to marry him, and Mary said yes. Not only that, but she was willing to go back with him to the Mabotsa mission.

David Livingstone realized he had a lot to be thankful for—even after being attacked by a lion!

Thankfulness is seeing God's goodness
even when bad things happen.

FROM GOD'S WORD:
We know that in everything God works for the good of those who love him. They are the people he called, because that was his plan (Romans 8:28).

LET'S TALK ABOUT IT:
1. Why did David Livingstone want to train African Christians to share the Good News?
2. Why would it have been easy to get discouraged? Why did Livingstone feel thankfulness instead?
3. What happens when we look for things to feel thankful about, even when something bad has happened?

HUMILITY
"Livingstone's Children"

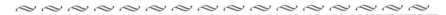

David Livingstone loved to explore! On his second great expedition, he traveled up the Zambeze River from the eastern coast of Africa.

But he worried about the slave trade developing in this area. Portuguese traders along the coast encouraged Africans called Red Caps (because of their red hats) to travel deep into Africa to buy slaves.

Slavery was common among African tribes, but the number of slaves was few. To make the numbers larger, the Red Caps tricked the tribes into fighting one another. Tribal war meant raids back and forth on villages. Many prisoners were taken. The Red Caps then bought these captives as slaves—from both sides.

Whenever David Livingstone came across a group of slaves, he chased off the Red Caps and freed the slaves. Several of the freed slaves chose to stay at Livingstone's mission station.

But the evil slave trade continued. "I must go deeper into the hills and carry the Gospel to people who have never heard," Livingstone decided. "Once they become Christians, they won't go to war so easily. And if I can get them to grow useful crops, they can sell the produce and will have no reason to sell slaves."

It seemed like a good plan. Using his ability to learn languages and his deep respect for the African people and their ways, Livingstone again traveled where no white person had ever gone. There were no slave traders here. He talked to people who had kept foreigners—white or black—out of their land for generations.

Then one day, he came upon a slave caravan that included people from some of these tribes. After he had chased off the Red Caps and freed the slaves, he asked, "How did the Red Caps get to you? You never let outsiders into your villages!"

"They said they were 'Livingstone's children,'" the people replied sadly. "So we thought they were safe and let them in."

David Livingstone was crushed. He had worked so hard to reach these tribes. Now that he was their friend, he had, without meaning to, opened the door for slave traders to come in, too! It was the very last thing he wanted to happen.

He became angry, and then his anger turned to despair. What could he do? He had failed. No, it was worse than failure. He had made things worse!

Many people might have quit and gone home at that point. But David did not quit. He did not think he was "too good" to fail. So he kept trying.

With humility, he continued his work doing the best he could to spread the Gospel, free slaves, and encourage the trade of produce, not slaves. Fifteen years after his death, the slave trade came to an end. His plan finally worked because he was not too proud to keep doing what was right, even when at first he had failed.

*Humility is not thinking you are so good that
you can't accept failure.*

FROM GOD'S WORD:

Because God has given me a special gift, I have
something to say to everyone among you. Do not
think you are better than you are. You must decide
what you really are by the amount of faith God has
given you (Romans 12:3).

LET'S TALK ABOUT IT:

1. How did the Red Caps get their slaves?
2. What was David Livingstone's plan to stop the
   slave trade?
3. Talk about a time when you failed at something
   and felt like quitting. What happened or what
   might have happened if you didn't quit?

DEDICATION
"Doctor Livingstone, I Presume?"

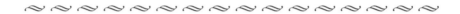

avid Livingstone's goal for his third expedition was to find where the great Nile River started. Africans said it ran out of a big lake in central Africa. So, again Livingstone headed into territory unknown to white people.

But years passed, and no one heard from David Livingstone. Finally people began to say he was dead. Henry Morton Stanley, an experienced newspaper reporter and traveler, also thought that Livingstone was probably dead. But his boss at the *New York Herald* did not agree.

"I don't care how much it costs," he said. "I want you to find David Livingstone or prove that he is dead. Either way it will make the greatest story of our day, and it will sell lots of papers. Now, go find him!"

David Livingstone traveled with a small number of friends and assistants. But Henry Stanley entered Africa with a group of two thousand men.

Livingstone always asked permission to pass peacefully

through African kingdoms, but Stanley fought like an invading army—and not without loss. Warfare, disease, and mutiny soon shrank his group to fifty-four men. Still, Stanley pushed on for seven months until, in November of 1871, he met two black men who greeted him in English.

"Who are you?" Stanley asked.

"I am Chuma, sir, the servant of Dr. Livingstone."

"And I am Susi," said the other African.

"How is the doctor?" asked Stanley.

"Not very well, sir."

"Then you better lead me to him."

Henry Stanley entered the town of Ujiji on Lake Tanganyika, and found David Livingstone resting in a mud hut. Stanley greeted him with the now-famous words, "Dr. Livingstone, I presume?"

Livingstone was sick from not having proper food and medicine. After helping him to get well, Stanley and Livingstone explored the northern end of Lake Tanganyika—but they did not find a river running out that might be the Nile. So Henry Stanley tried to convince the doctor to return to England.

"No," said Livingstone. "I still have work to do here." (He never did find the source of the Nile. John Hanning Speke later discovered that it flowed out of Lake Victoria, many miles to the northeast.)

Once again Stanley tried to convince the old doctor to give up and return home.

"Africa is where my heart is," said David Livingstone. "I love the people. But I will send these letters back to England with you."

Soon Henry Stanley went back to America and became famous for his stories of finding David Livingstone.

Livingstone explored Africa for two more years with Chuma,

who had been rescued from the Red Caps twenty years earlier, and Susi. When David Livingstone died, his faithful friends buried his heart beneath a tree because "his heart was in Africa." Then they wrapped his body with spices and cloth to preserve it, and Chuma took it all the way to England for burial.

Dedication is totally committing your life
to a God-given task or goal.

FROM GOD'S WORD:

Therefore, since we are surrounded by such a great cloud of witnesses, let us throw off everything that hinders and the sin that so easily entangles, and let us run with perseverance the race marked out for us (Hebrews 12:1, NIV).

LET'S TALK ABOUT IT:

1. How was the way David Livingstone traveled different from Stanley's?
2. Why didn't Livingstone want to go back to England with Henry Morton Stanley?
3. Tell about something very hard that you kept working at until you finished.

MARTIN LUTHER

Giant of the Reformation

Martin Luther was born on November 10, 1483, in Eisleben, Germany. As a young man, lightning nearly struck him, and he promised to become a monk if God would keep him safe.

He made good on his promise and entered a monastery. On April 3, 1507, Luther was ordained a priest and later became a professor at the University of Wittenberg.

Still, Luther felt troubled by his sins. He felt as if God were unhappy with him. The harder he worked to be "good," the worse he felt—until one day he read Romans 1:17: "The just shall live by faith" (NKJV).

He had not realized that he could not *earn* God's favor. It was a gift from God that he could have only by faith. After Luther accepted God's gift, his first question was, "Why didn't I learn this from my church?"

He looked around. The church told people that to please God they must buy "indulgences" (written pardons for sin) and obey church rules. This brought money into the church treasury and kept the people under control for the government. But it was a trick.

Luther first tried to convince church leaders that they had to teach the truth. A few agreed, and Duke Frederick of Saxony sympathized. But most church and state leaders saw Luther's ideas as a threat to their power.

Luther's trial in the city of Worms was the last straw. He refused to take back what he had written unless the Bible proved him wrong. He might have been executed if Duke Frederick had not protected him.

Martin Luther died in 1546, but his church reforms lived on as the Lutheran church.

VISION
Saved for a Purpose

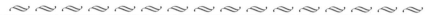

oing to see a girl?" Martin Luther's friend teased as the two college students set off on their three-day trip home.

"Who said anything about a girl? This is vacation," said young Martin.

"Of course, and I'm *sure* you'll spend the whole time studying for exams." His friend gave him a playful push.

Martin lunged back as his friend darted out of reach. Martin charged after him but took only a couple steps when his toe caught under a root and he fell headfirst into the dust.

He didn't jump up. Pain ripped through his leg. A dark stain spread down his hose. He was carrying a double-edged sword as protection against robbers. But without a sheath to cover it, it had caught and sliced his leg.

The blood flowed freely, and Martin couldn't stop it.

"What's the matter? Let's go," called his friend.

Martin thought he might die, and words wouldn't come.

In a few moments, his friend knelt down by his side. "That's a bad cut! I better go back to Erfurt and get some help."

Help came, and strong arms carried Martin back to the university, where a doctor finally stopped the bleeding. But Martin's life hung in the balance for several days before he recovered.

A short time later, a typhoid plague swept through the city. The sickness took the lives of several friends and classmates.

Life is not certain, thought Martin. *It could be me on that deathbed.* Then what? Would God let him into heaven?

He vowed to be a better person and buy a few extra indulgences from the priests. Maybe that would make God happy with him.

At age twenty-one, he graduated and decided to go on for a doctor of law degree. But he took a break and went home for ten days. On his way back, a violent summer storm blew up. The sky boiled with clouds, and the afternoon became so dark that he almost needed a lantern to find his way.

Fear gripped Martin's heart. He couldn't shake the notion that devils and goblins were mocking him from behind trees or out of the swirling clouds.

When huge raindrops began to fall, he dashed under a large elm tree. As soon as he reached its shelter, a mighty bolt of lightning split the tree in half. Its jagged skeleton blazed against the angry sky.

"Oh, God," wailed Martin as he fell to his knees. "Save me! Have mercy on me, and I will serve you forever."

As with most summer storms, this one passed quickly, and brilliant sunshine stabbed through the clouds, bringing relief and hope.

Martin realized he had been saved from death three times. He did not forget his promise, and within two weeks he went to a monastery to become a monk.

He knew he was alive for some purpose. He did not want

God to have to find someone else to fulfill that purpose.

*Vision includes recognizing that God has a
purpose for your life and every person's life.*

FROM GOD'S WORD:
Now this is what the LORD says. . . . "Don't be afraid,
because I have saved you. I have called you by
name, and you are mine" (Isaiah 43:1).

LET'S TALK ABOUT IT:
1. Was Martin wrong to think he might die anytime?
2. Why did he decide to become a monk?
3. Even though you may not know what God wants
   you to do, how can you know that He has a
   purpose for you?

COURAGE
"Here I Stand!"

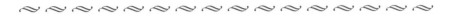

artin Luther could not keep quiet. He was angry at the church officials who tried to fool people by selling them pieces of paper (indulgences) that said their sins—past and future—were forgiven.

When Luther had traveled to Rome, he had seen the luxuries the clergy had bought with these poor people's money. A piece of paper couldn't forgive sins! He had also discovered how wicked some popes and other leaders had become. For centuries, they had controlled people and nations. One pope was even accused of poisoning the pope before him!

With its priests and popes doing so many sinful things, how could the Roman Church promise forgiveness to anyone? Besides, Luther had seen in the Bible that no one could earn or buy God's favor: "The just shall live by faith" and faith alone. He knew Christians could only live good lives when they trusted Jesus Christ to help them.

He had to do something! So, on October 31, 1517, Martin Luther nailed a list of ninety-five objections (or "theses") to the door of the Castle Church in Wittenberg. He began writing books and pamphlets telling about church wrongdoings.

These actions made many church and state leaders angry. Luther had challenged their power and uncovered their evil ways. He could not be ignored.

Luther's enemies tried to force him to stand trial in Rome. But friends, such as Duke Frederick of Saxony, knew this was dangerous. If he went to Rome, Luther would likely be killed. Instead, they arranged for his trial to take place in Germany in the city of Worms. The Emperor Charles V would be there to oversee the trial.

Dr. John Eck, a famous Roman Catholic scholar, was chosen to prosecute Martin Luther.

At the trial, Eck placed a pile of Martin Luther's books on the table. "Will you give up these teachings?" asked Eck.

Luther asked for some time to prepare a proper answer. The next day, he said that much of what he had written was the simple truth. No one would argue with it. "So there is no reason to give that part up.

"Some of my other writings deal with the awful abuses of the Roman Church here in Germany. And everyone knows those problems are real, so that truth cannot be set aside.

"Besides," he continued, "God made our minds free, so one's conscience (beliefs about what is right or wrong) cannot be forced. That's my answer."

"Very clever," said Eck. "Now give me a simple answer."

"All right," agreed Martin Luther. "Unless I can be convinced by the clear teachings of the Bible that I am wrong, I cannot and I will not retract what I have written. Here I stand. I cannot do otherwise. God help me. Amen!"

Courage sometimes means risking your own safety to do what is right.

FROM GOD'S WORD:

Be alert. Continue strong in the faith. Have courage, and be strong (1 Corinthians 16:13).

LET'S TALK ABOUT IT:

1. Why did Martin Luther believe it was wrong for the Roman Church to sell indulgences?
2. How does the Bible say we can find forgiveness of our sins?
3. When have you needed courage to do what was right?

JOY

Wife in a Barrel

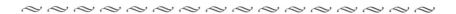

ear Dr. Luther," the letter began. "We are twelve nuns in the convent near Grimma. We understand you no longer believe we are bound by the vows we took when we came to live at the convent. Would you help us escape?"

Martin Luther scratched his head. What had he started?

As a priest in the Roman Church, Luther had taken a vow of celibacy (to not marry). But reading the Bible made him see that this was not required. In saying that overseers or bishops should be "the husband of only one wife," the Bible clearly allowed for church leaders to marry. Even the apostle Peter, whom the Roman Church thought of as its first pope, had had a wife.

So Luther wrote about these new beliefs.

In Germany, nearly one-fifth of the population lived in convents and monasteries where marriage was not allowed. Many became nuns or monks because they hoped it would help them to become holy. Others had been forced into it by hard times. Luther did not think this was good.

As the Reformation went on, the church in Germany became

more and more separate from the church in Rome. Martin Luther had translated the New Testament into German so the average person could now read the Bible. Worship services were being said in German instead of Latin. And many other changes happened.

Now some nuns wanted out of their convent.

Luther asked an old friend for help. The friend made a plan to smuggle the nuns out in empty herring barrels. The cartload of fishy-smelling nuns arrived in Wittenberg, but they were still not safe. If they returned to their family homes, their superiors from the convent would find them and take them back. And the families would probably cooperate.

Marriage was the only answer. Surprisingly, husbands were soon found for all but one of the nuns. Her name was Katherine von Bora. "I will have none other than Martin Luther himself," she declared.

The next time Luther visited his parents, he told them the story of this daring young woman as a joke.

"Well, why not marry her?" his father asked seriously.

"Not me!" said Luther. "My enemies would use it against me."

"I told you that you should not become a monk," his father reminded him. "How will the family name continue if you do not marry and have children?"

Martin Luther thought about what his father had said. On June 15, 1525, Luther and Katherine were quietly married.

Two weeks later, they planned a wedding feast to celebrate. When Luther wrote to a friend to invite him to the feast, he said, "I have made the angels laugh and the devils weep."

It was a great party, and a year later their first son was born. When Martin Luther looked down into the cradle, he grinned like any proud papa. "Kick away, my boy," he said. "The pope tied me down in diapers, too, but I kicked them off."

*Joy is to be found when you don't take life
or yourself too seriously.*

FROM GOD'S WORD:
A cheerful look brings joy to the heart, and good news gives health to the bones (Proverbs 15:30 NIV).

LET'S TALK ABOUT IT:
1. What were some of the changes that Martin Luther thought should happen in church life?
2. Why do you think the nuns might have wanted out of their convent?
3. Tell about a time when a little humor made a hard time easier.

DWIGHT L. MOODY

Shoe Salesman for God

As a young man, Dwight Moody's dream was to get rich.
Born February 5, 1837, in Northfield, Massachusetts, he left home
at age seventeen to work for his uncle in Boston as a shoe salesman. Dwight was a natural salesman, and at age twenty landed a
job in Chicago with C. E. Wisell, the shoe tycoon.

But young Dwight Moody also cared for the kids in Chicago's
slums. He helped set up a Sunday school, which in time grew into
the Illinois Street Independent Church. After a few years he gave
up selling shoes forever, because "selling kids on God" was much
more exciting.

The Young Man's Christian Association (YMCA) appointed
Dwight Moody as a missionary. In 1867, while Moody was speaking at YMCAs in England, Rev. Henry Varley challenged him with
these words: "The world has yet to see what God can do with one
man wholly dedicated to Him." These words inspired Moody. He
decided to become that man—he would give his whole life to
God!

In 1870, at a YMCA International Convention, he heard a hymn singer with a wonderful voice. He invited this man, Ira Sankey, to join him as music director. For the next twenty years, "Moody and Sankey" were a world famous team for God.

On October 8, 1871, the Great Chicago Fire destroyed Moody's home, the YMCA, *and* the Illinois Street Church. But Dwight Moody saw the destruction of his work in Chicago as an opportunity—now he could work to tell even more people the Gospel. The time of the great evangelistic campaigns began.

Even though Moody had little schooling, he started Northfield Seminary for Girls and Mount Herman School for Boys in Massachusetts, and helped begin a Bible school for lay men and women in Chicago. Only after Moody's death was it renamed the Moody Bible Institute.

Just before the turn of the century, his weak heart forced him to cut short an evangelistic trip. Only sixty-two, Dwight Moody died December 22, 1899, at his home in Northfield, where he is buried.

REPENTANCE
More Fun Than Selling Shoes!

~~~~~~~~~~~~~~~~~~~~~~~~~~~~~~~~~~~

No one—absolutely no one—could fill up a Sunday school better than young Dwight Moody. All week long, he worked as a shoe salesman for one of the biggest shoe companies in Chicago. (He was *good* at selling shoes, too, and he planned to make a lot of money.) But on Sunday, he walked through the streets rounding up as many kids as he could. He took them all to Sunday school.

Once he got them there, though, Moody felt like his job was done. It was someone else's job to teach the Bible, wasn't it? He was sure of it the day Mr. Hibbert was sick and Moody was asked to teach his class of twelve-year-old girls. Those girls acted up during the whole lesson—even laughed in his face! Moody had to bite his tongue to keep from telling them to "get out and don't come back."

One day, Mr. Hibbert came into the shoe store and asked to speak to Moody. The man was only middle-aged, but he was sick with a rattling cough.

"How can I help you, Mr. H?" Moody said. "You look like you should be in bed."

Mr. Hibbert nodded sadly. "My lungs are bleeding . . . doctor says I won't survive another winter in Chicago. So I'm leaving soon to go back home to my family—going home to die, I suppose. But—"

"But what, Mr. H?" Moody asked.

"I hate leaving my class," said the Sunday school teacher. "You see, not one of those girls has accepted Christ as her Savior yet. If I leave them now . . ."

Oh no! thought Moody. *He's not going to ask me to teach that class of horrible girls, is he?* Quickly he said, "Why don't you go visit them—you know, individually—and tell them how you feel."

Mr. Hibbert's tired face lit up. "That's exactly what I want to do, Dwight. But . . . I don't know if I have the strength. Will you go with me?"

Moody gladly agreed. The least he could do for the poor man was take him where he needed to go.

So each evening after work, Dwight Moody walked with Mr. Hibbert to each girl's house, helped him up the rickety stairs to the dingy apartments, and sat quietly while the teacher talked sincerely to each pupil. To Moody's amazement, first one, then another, then *another* girl accepted Christ as her Savior!

After ten days of visiting, every single girl in that class had given her life to Jesus. On the last day before Mr. Hibbert was supposed to leave, Moody picked up all the girls so they could say goodbye to their teacher. It turned into a regular prayer meeting, as each girl tearfully thanked God for her teacher and prayed for him.

Moody went to the train station the next day to see Mr. Hibbert off. To his surprise, all the girls showed up too, crying and waving as the train pulled out. Mr. Hibbert stood on the platform at the back of the train, a peaceful smile on his face. His finger pointed up toward heaven, where he would see each of his students again someday.

Dwight Moody's heart was full nearly to the bursting point. "Oh, God!" he cried. "Selling shoes and making money don't seem very important compared to what I've seen in the last two weeks. Forgive me, Lord, for focusing on the wrong things. From now on, I want to tell boys and girls and men and women about the Good News. I'm your man full time!"

Repentance is not just saying you're sorry for sin,
but going in a new direction.

FROM GOD'S WORD:
Come near to God, and God will come near to you. You sinners, clean sin out of your lives. You who are trying to follow God and the world at the same time, make your thinking pure (James 4:8).

LET'S TALK ABOUT IT:
1. Dwight Moody was already a Christian and bringing kids to Sunday school. Why did he need to repent?
2. In the verse above, what does it mean to try to "follow God and the world at the same time"?
3. What are some things in your life that might cause you to follow the world and keep you from sharing the Good News with others?

BOLDNESS
The Night Chicago Burned

Dwight Moody looked around the packed YMCA meeting room at the men, women, and children who had come to hear him preach. "Ask yourself, 'What shall I do with Jesus?'" he said again. The people were restless—the streets outside seemed alive with running footsteps and faraway shouts. He wondered if anyone was paying attention.

"Go back home and think about that question this week," he urged. "Then come back next Sunday and tell me what you're going to do with Jesus. Mr. Sankey—lead us in a song."

Dwight Moody turned the meeting over to his song leader. Ira Sankey's rich baritone voice never failed to draw people into enthusiastic singing. Except tonight. Everyone seemed distracted by a change in the air, a strange color in the sky outside the windows, and church bells ringing. Sankey began the third verse of the hymn:

Today the Savior calls;
For refuge fly;

The storm of justice falls,
And death is nigh.

But few people were singing. When Moody dismissed the meeting, he and Sankey went outside to see what was going on. Just then a team of horses pulling a fire wagon galloped furiously down the street. In the distance, the skyline was lit by a savage orange glow.

Chicago was on fire! Not just a few buildings, but whole sections of the city!

Ira went back inside the YMCA building to rescue a few valuable items, while Moody hurried to the Illinois Street Church— the church which had grown up around the Sunday school mission he had started years earlier. By the time Dwight Moody reached home, where his wife Emily and two children were waiting anxiously for him, both the YMCA and the Illinois Street Church were in flames.

But the fire seemed to be moving in a different direction, so the Moody family went to bed and tried to sleep. But soon after midnight, they heard pounding on their front door. "Get out! Get out!" cried the police. "The fire is coming this way!"

A neighbor made room for the Moodys' two children in their carriage as they escaped from the city. Dwight and Emily Moody had to escape on foot, pushing a baby buggy with a few of their belongings.

When the fire finally burned itself out, three hundred people had died, seventeen thousand buildings had been destroyed, and ninety thousand people were homeless—including the Moody family.

"Emily," Moody said huskily as they looked at the heap of ashes that had been their home, "I made a big mistake."

Was her husband remembering some special thing he had not saved from the flames?

No, Dwight Moody was thinking of something else. "I gave the people a week to think about what they were going to do with Jesus," he said sadly. "But they didn't have a week. Never again will I miss a chance to ask people, 'What are you going to do with Jesus *today?*' "

Boldness in telling others about Jesus comes when you realize that asking Jesus to be your Savior can't always wait until "tomorrow."

FROM GOD'S WORD:
I tell you that the "right time" is now, and the "day of salvation" is now (2 Corinthians 6:2b).

LET'S TALK ABOUT IT:
1. Why do you think Dwight Moody gave his listeners a week to think about what they were going to do with Jesus?
2. Why did Dwight say he would never do that again?
3. Is there someone you have been wanting to talk to about Jesus? Pray that God will give you the boldness to talk to that person soon!

STRENGTH
"The Ship Is Sinking!"

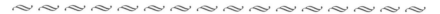

apa, you really have to quit working so hard," said Will Moody. "The doctor said that if you don't slow down, you're going to kill yourself."

"Mmmph," muttered Dwight Moody. He was lying in his bunk on the steamer *Spree*, crossing the Atlantic Ocean from England to America. As usual, he was feeling seasick. Could the doctor be right? Moody was only fifty-four, but he was very overweight, and he had been feeling tired lately. But how could he slow down? Why, the World's Fair was coming to Chicago the next year in 1893—and he was planning a six-month-long evangelistic campaign to reach all the people who were coming to the fair. But maybe others could do most of the preaching. Maybe—

Just then there was a loud boom, and the ship shuddered violently. Will rushed up on deck to see what had happened and came back with awful news: "Papa, the ship's drive shaft has broken. Water is coming into the ship—I think we're sinking!"

Frightened passengers were gathering on the deck. The stern of the ship was riding low in the water. Rough seas tossed the boat from side to side. The captain and the crew debated what to do.

Stay on the ship, or lower lifeboats into the rough water? For now they decided to stay on the ship, sending up signal flares, hoping that another ship would rescue them.

The first night was terrible. No one slept. All the passengers crowded together in the ship's lounge. Even Dwight Moody struggled. He was not afraid to die; he knew he would go to heaven to be with Jesus. But to never see his wife and other children again on this earth . . . to leave so much work undone. . . . He later wrote, "It was the darkest hour of my life!"

The next morning, Moody got permission to have a worship service in the salon. He read Psalm 107:23–28: "Others went out to sea in ships. . . . In their misery they cried out to the LORD, and he saved them from their troubles." Also Psalm 91:11, "He has put his angels in charge of you to watch over you wherever you go." Many people were comforted—including Dwight Moody himself. Whether he died now or later, it was up to the Lord. God's will was all that mattered.

That night Moody went to bed and immediately fell asleep. In the middle of the night, Will shook his father awake. "Come and look!" the young man said excitedly.

Up on deck, they could see the lights of a ship coming toward them. It was another steamer, the *Lake Huron*. In spite of the rough seas, cables were attached between the two ships. The danger wasn't over yet, but somehow the *Huron* managed to tow the crippled *Spree* all the way back to England. It took eight days.

Rejoicing in their safety, Dwight decided God must have a reason for sparing his life. "I can't slow down now!" he told Will. "God has work for me to do! Hundreds of thousands of people are coming to the World's Fair in Chicago—and they all need a Savior. And if God has work for me to do, He will give me the strength to do it."

Strength is the power God gives you to finish a job,
even when you feel weak.

FROM GOD'S WORD:

But he said to me, "My grace is enough for you. When you are weak, my power is made perfect in you" (2 Corinthians 12:9).

LET'S TALK ABOUT IT:

1. How did Dwight Moody feel when he thought the ship was sinking?
2. Why did Moody think God wanted him to keep working hard and preaching to people every day (even against the doctor's orders)?
3. Have you ever asked God to give you the strength to do something for Him, even when you felt weak or powerless? What happened?

SAMUEL MORRIS

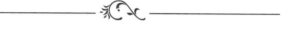

Evangelist From Africa

Prince Kaboo was born in 1872 in Liberia (western Africa). His father was king of the Kru tribe during a war with the neighboring Grebos. The Grebos won.

Because the king could not pay his war taxes, he had to surrender Kaboo as a "pawn" until the debt was paid. This happened once when Kaboo was a small child, but his father was able to free him quickly. However, when Kaboo was a young teenager, new fighting broke out. His people were defeated, and he was again taken as a pawn.

When Kaboo's father was unable to pay his ransom, the Grebos began torturing Kaboo to force his father to pay.

Once when Kaboo was being whipped, a blinding light flashed, and a voice from heaven said, "Rise up and run."

Strength returned to Kaboo's wounded body, and he ran into the jungle. Grebo warriors followed him until dark.

But nighttime did not stop Kaboo. God provided a miraculous light to guide him. During the day, he slept in hollow logs.

Finally, he arrived at the town of Monrovia, where missionaries told him about Jesus.

When Kaboo heard the story of Saul's conversion on the road to Damascus, he exclaimed, "That happened to me, too. A light flashed, and God spoke from heaven."

Kaboo (called Samuel Morris by then) went to the United States to study God's Word at Taylor University in Fort Wayne, Indiana. Whenever he spoke at the university or while traveling, powerful revivals broke out. Many people gave their hearts to Jesus.

However, weeks of being tortured had weakened Samuel's body. During the harsh winter of 1892–93 he became ill. He died that spring.

Though Samuel's death at the age of twenty seemed tragic, God used it to inspire many students to be missionaries in Samuel's place. A Taylor University Bible School was even started in Africa.

PEACEMAKER
The "Sheriff" of the Three-Masted Ship

he tough sea captain didn't want this young African boy on board his ship.

"But my Father told me you would take me to New York," said Samuel Morris. "I'm going there to learn about the Holy Spirit."

"Get away from here," the captain growled. He kicked Samuel.

But the next day, the boy was back, declaring confidently that he was going on the ship. Samuel wouldn't give up, so finally the captain gave in.

Samuel had no skills as a sailor, and because of his black skin, he was hated by the crew. But one crew member accepted him. The captain's cabin boy had just been seriously hurt and could not get up. Samuel knelt down and prayed for him. Immediately, the young man rose to his feet, completely healed.

One day when most of the crew was drunk, a fight broke out. A large Malay man thought someone had insulted him; he charged at his shipmates, swinging a cutlass.

Samuel stepped in his way and said, "Don't kill! Don't kill!"

The Malay man hated blacks and had killed others in the past. He'd sworn to kill Samuel, too. But for some reason, he slowly lowered his weapon and went below deck. Every man on deck was shocked. They knew how violent the man was. Samuel had a power stronger than the meanest sailor!

Unlike the sheriffs of the American "Old West," Samuel didn't threaten anyone in order to restore peace. Instead, he immediately began praying for all the men who were fighting. Before the captain knew what he was doing, he was praying, too, and confessing his own sins. That same day, he asked Jesus to be his Savior.

By the next morning, the murderous Malay was so sick that no one expected him to live. But Samuel was not discouraged. He went to visit the man and prayed for him, even though this was the man who had said he would kill him. God answered Samuel's prayer. The Malay man recovered immediately. From that time on, he treated Samuel like a brother.

Samuel started holding church services on deck, and every man happily took part. Samuel's faith had changed the whole spirit of the ship.

Years later, when the captain of this ship learned that Samuel Morris had died, he was so sad that he could not speak for some time. Then he said that most of the old crew were still on board and excited to find out about their beloved hero and minister. After all, he had changed life on that ship. Before he came aboard, no one had ever prayed out loud, but after Samuel shared the Gospel with them, they became like one family—a family that could talk to their Father.

Peacemaking sometimes means being willing to risk your safety in order to prevent harm to others.

FROM GOD'S WORD:

People who work for peace in a peaceful way plant a good crop of right-living (James 3:18).

LET'S TALK ABOUT IT:

1. At first, why didn't the sailors welcome Samuel Morris as part of the crew? What changed their minds?
2. Why did Samuel risk his own safety to stop the man with the cutlass?
3. Tell about a time when you tried to break up a fight or settle an argument between two people.

BOLDNESS
Taking New York

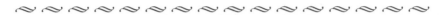

he tired missionary had been talking to Samuel Morris at the mission in Monrovia for hours. "If you want to learn any more about the Holy Spirit," she finally said, "then you'll have to go see Stephen Merritt in New York."

So, at about the age of nineteen, Samuel left his home in Liberia and talked his way on board a ship bound for New York.

Besides being a Bible teacher and well-known preacher, Merritt ran a mission for homeless people. When Samuel stepped off the ship and onto the dock in New York, he boldly said to the first person he met, "Please take me to Stephen Merritt." He had no idea how big New York City was!

But even though the mission was on the other side of town, this man had stayed there often and agreed to show Samuel the way.

When Samuel met Stephen Merritt, he explained, "I have come from Africa to talk with you about the Holy Spirit."

"I'm sorry, son," said Merritt, "but right now I'm going out the door to a prayer meeting. Wait in the mission. When I get back,

I'll see about a place for you to sleep."

Stephen Merritt forgot about his new guest until he returned late that night. In the mission, he found Samuel with seventeen men around him. They were some of the toughest street men Merritt had ever housed, but Samuel had them on their knees praying and asking for God's forgiveness.

That Friday evening was just the beginning.

On Saturday, Merritt was scheduled to speak at a funeral. He invited Samuel to go along with him, thinking he would show this bright young African around the city and introduce him to some important people.

After seeing the opera house, Central Park, and several other sights, Samuel said, "Stephen Merritt, do you ever pray in this coach?"

"Oh yes," said Merritt, "I often find it a fine place to pray as I drive about."

"Good," said Samuel, and he *knelt* down and began to pray. "Dear Father, I have come all the way from Africa to talk to Mr. Merritt about your Holy Spirit, but all he wants to do is show me other things. Please take these *things* out of his heart so he cannot talk of anything except your Holy Spirit."

Merritt was shocked, but their conversation changed. As they talked, the power of the Holy Spirit seemed to fill the coach. At the funeral, the message Merritt had prepared left his mind, and instead he preached what the Holy Spirit gave him to say. When it was over, many people gave their lives to Jesus.

Later, Merritt said that even though important church leaders had prayed over him, he had never felt the power of the Holy Spirit so strongly as he had in that coach with Samuel.

On Sunday, Merritt invited Samuel to speak to a Sunday school class of young people. At first they laughed. But when Merritt returned to the room after a short time away, he found the young people crying over their past sins and praying to God for forgiveness.

Those young people organized the Samuel Morris Missionary Society, which helped support Samuel when he left New York to study at Taylor University.

Boldness requires going after a goal single-mindedly.

FROM GOD'S WORD:
Ask, and God will give to you. Search, and you will find. Knock, and the door will open for you (Matthew 7:7).

LET'S TALK ABOUT IT:
1. How did God answer Samuel Morris's search to know more about the Holy Spirit?
2. Who benefitted from Samuel's boldness?
3. What is a goal in your life that you think God would bless if you went after it boldly?

ENCOURAGEMENT
Take Heart!

~~~~~~~~~~~~~~~~~~~~~~~~~~~~~~~~~~~~~

I am Samuel Morris. I have just come from Africa with a message for your people," the young student said as he stepped onto the church platform.

The surprised minister didn't know what to do. He would not usually let a stranger take over his service. But something about the young African caused him to agree.

It was Samuel's first Sunday in Fort Wayne, Indiana, where he had come to attend Taylor University. He did not have a prepared sermon. He simply started praying and encouraged the people to do the same. Soon the whole congregation was on their knees praying and worshiping God. "It was the most joyful service we ever had," said the grateful minister later.

After that, Samuel spoke in other churches—even in a roller-skating rink. People came from all over to hear him talk about God.

Though he was just learning to read, those who heard him speak were surprised at the freshness and strength of his messages. One said, "He spoke for forty minutes in a quiet yet earnest style, simple and natural as a child. Everyone was interested."

At school, Samuel did not eat any food or drink any water from Thursday night until Saturday morning. He had figured out that God had miraculously rescued him from his Grebo captors on a Friday. So he saved that day for praying—"talking to my Father," as he called it.

As other people heard about this young African at the school, they gave money to a "faith fund" for his costs. (Even after Samuel's death, that fund continued to grow, helping one hundred needy students who were preparing for mission work.)

During Samuel's time at Taylor University, the people in charge of the school almost closed it because there was not enough money to pay the bills.

"Take heart," said Samuel, "and pray." Inspired by his faith, the board members turned to God for help.

At their next meeting, one board member suggested that if the school couldn't afford to remain in Fort Wayne, it should move to Upland. Move the whole school? That seemed impossible! But with Samuel's encouragement, the board member raised enough money *within one day* to purchase new land and move the school.

Samuel's inspiration meant new life for the school. But at age twenty, Samuel became ill because of the injuries he had received as a boy in Africa. After his death, hundreds attended his funeral, packing the church and spilling out into the street. In Samuel, many of them had seen and learned more about faith and the power of God to save people than they had ever known before.

Encouraged by Samuel's example, many students volunteered as missionaries in his place. And for years to come, missions was an important focus of the school—until hundreds had gone overseas to be missionaries.

Of Samuel Morris, the president of the university said, "He thought he was coming over here to prepare himself for his mission to his people, but his coming was to prepare Taylor University for her mission to the whole world."

Encouragement helps others do more than they think they can do.

FROM GOD'S WORD:
You should meet together and encourage each other. Do this even more as you see the day coming (Hebrews 10:25).

LET'S TALK ABOUT IT:
1. How did Samuel Morris encourage the first church he went to in Fort Wayne?
2. How did his encouragement save the university?
3. Tell about a time when someone encouraged you to do more than you thought you could do.

GEORGE MÜLLER

————————— ❦ —————————

Man of Faith

At the age of sixteen, George Müller landed in jail. He had wasted his father's money by drinking and gambling.

When his father heard the news, he was angry. George had been born in Kroppenstadt, Germany, on September 27, 1805. His father paid for his education, hoping he would become a Lutheran minister. But when George went away to school, he became a playboy.

Jail did not reform him. When he got out, he went back to his wild life. Then one day a friend convinced George to come to a prayer meeting and Bible study. There George Müller gave his life to Jesus.

In 1829, he moved to England and settled in the country. He joined the Plymouth Brethren church and became a preacher. Müller was so good at being a preacher that the little congregation soon grew from 18 members to 227.

Müller came to believe the Lord wanted him to pray for the money he needed and not to ask people for it.

In 1835, George Müller opened an orphanage in the city of Bristol for poor children. Until then, only rich children were accepted in England's few orphanages. Poor children were left on the streets or sent to cruel workhouses.

Müller had two reasons for starting the orphanages: He wanted to care for the children, and he wanted to show that God would supply anyone's needs who prayed and trusted only in Him.

When the house in Bristol became too crowded, Müller used money God supplied to purchase some out-of-town property, known as Ashley Downs. There he built five huge houses that were home to two thousand children at a time.

And just as Müller had believed, God miraculously provided everything from food to money for building.

During his life, which ended on March 10, 1898, George Müller housed, educated, and trained over ten thousand boys and girls.

FAITH
Breakfast From Heaven

~~~~~~

Abigail Townsend was not an orphan, but when her family moved to Bristol, England, a close friendship developed between her father and George Müller. Abbie often went out to Ashley Downs with her father to visit the orphanage. She grew very fond of the kind gentleman who ran it.

One morning, Müller took Abbie by the hand and said, "Come, see what our Father in heaven will do for us today."

He led her into the long dining room, where bowls and cups were on the table, but there was no food. There was also no food in the kitchen and no money to buy food. But the orphan children were standing behind their seats, respectfully waiting for breakfast to begin.

"Children," said Müller, "it will soon be time for school, so let's pray. Dear Father, we thank you for what you are going to give us to eat."

Just then a knock sounded at the door, and there stood the local baker. "Mr. Müller," he said, "I couldn't sleep last night. Somehow I felt you didn't have bread for breakfast, and the Lord wanted me to send you some. So I got up at two o'clock and baked some fresh bread for you."

Müller thanked the baker and praised God for His care. "Children," he said, "we not only have bread, but God has given us the rare treat of *fresh* bread."

Right away there came a second knock at the door. This time it was the milkman, who announced that his cart had broken down outside the orphanage. "I must empty my wagon before I can repair it. Could the children use my cans of fresh milk?"

There, before her very eyes, little Abbie saw God provide fresh bread and milk for the children.

"I wish God would answer my prayers like He does yours, Mr. Müller," said Abigail.

"Oh, He will," said George Müller. "All you have to do is ask Him. Now, what is it you want?"

"Some wool yarn," said Abbie, grinning.

"Well, let's pray, then." And Müller helped her to say a short prayer.

Some time later, Abbie came running back to Müller. "I want to pray again," she said.

"God heard you the first time, child. You don't need to pester Him."

"But I forgot to tell Him what color I want," said Abbie.

Taking her up on his knee, he said, "You are right, you should tell God exactly what you want."

"Please, God," prayed Abbie, "send mixed colors." Then she jumped down and ran off to play.

The next morning, a package arrived for Abigail. Her Sunday school teacher had forgotten her birthday and sent a late gift . . . of mixed colors of yarn!

Faith includes the confidence that God hears
and answers your prayers.

FROM GOD'S WORD:

"If you believe, you will get anything you ask for in prayer" (Matthew 21:22).

LET'S TALK ABOUT IT

1. Why did George Müller thank God for the children's breakfast when there was no food on the table or in the kitchen?
2. How did God answer Abbie's prayer?
3. Does God always answer our prayers exactly the way we ask them? Talk about how God has answered prayer in your life.

GRACIOUSNESS
The Unwelcome Gift

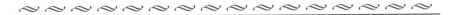

One day, a good-hearted man sent George Müller a check for 100 pounds (about $200). The letter with the check said, "I think it right that some money should be provided for you. Though this is just a beginning, I hope many good Christians will add to it to form a fund to support you and your family."

But George Müller did not think that was the way God wanted him to work. In fact, he felt this was a temptation to trust in a bank account instead of in God. But he knew the man had not meant his gift to be a temptation, so he was gracious and kind in his reply.

"My dear Sir," Müller wrote, "thank you for your kind letter and the check. However, I have no property of any kind, and neither does my wife. Nor have I received one single shilling of regular salary for the last twenty-six years. When I am in need of anything, I fall on my knees and ask God if He would please give it to me. He then puts it in the heart of someone or other to help me.

"In this way, all my wants have been completely supplied

during the last twenty-six years. I can say, to the praise of God, I have lacked nothing. My wife and our only daughter agree. We are not tired of this way of living. In fact, we find it to be better day by day.

"I have never thought it necessary to save for the future or look out for myself or my family except that we trust God. So, when we see someone in need—an old woman, a sick person, or a helpless infant—I freely give whatever I have at the time. I know that later, when I am in need, God will provide for me. I don't need to look out for myself in any way other than to trust in Him.

"Therefore, I am unable to accept your generous gift toward setting up a regular support fund for us, and so I am returning your check.

"Anything given to me or the work of God, I thankfully accept if I can use it or pass it on as God directs. But your gift seemed to have the plan of making me less dependent on God's daily care for me. To accept it would lead me to begin trusting in the fund, possibly more than in God.

"Nevertheless, I appreciate your kindness and pray that God would richly bless you. I am, dear Sir, Yours very gratefully, George Müller."

Graciousness includes not putting down someone
who means you no harm.

FROM GOD'S WORD:
Let your speech always be with grace, seasoned with salt, that you may know how you ought to answer each one (Colossians 4:6, NKJV).

LET'S TALK ABOUT IT:

1. What did the man who sent George Müller the money want him to do with it?

2. Why did George return the money? What did he think was a better way to live?

3. Tell about a time when someone wanted to give you something or invited you to do something that you knew might not be best for you, even though that person was trying to be friendly or kind. How did you respond?

TRUST
Will the Boiler Blow?

~~~~~~~~~~~~~~~~~~~~~~~~~~~~~~~~~~

Usually George Müller told only God about his needs. Afterward, he told people how faithfully God had provided for him.

However, one Friday afternoon in November, Müller did report a need before God answered. "This is an emergency that no person can help with," he announced at lunch. "So I can tell you children about it *before* God answers. I am asking all of you to pray.

"The furnace boiler in House Number One has suddenly started to leak. It is a very bad leak, and winter is coming soon. If we don't repair it, the heat will fail, and the little children who live there will get cold. What's worse, if the boiler should go dry, it could blow up."

Müller then went on to explain that the brick wall around the furnace made it impossible to replace or repair the boiler without tearing down the wall. Such a big project would take several days to complete.

"The repairs will begin next Wednesday," he explained. "But, as you can see," and he pointed out the window, "a storm is coming. So, I'm asking you to pray with me for two things: that God would change this cold north wind into a warm south wind, and that He would give the workmen a mind to work so the job can be completed quickly."

That was Friday. Saturday and Sunday the cold wind blew harder. Monday and Tuesday were no better. In fact, by Tuesday night the sky looked heavy with snow about to fall, and the wind howled.

But the next morning, the children awoke to warm sunshine. The wind was blowing from the south! It felt like spring instead of the beginning of winter.

The whole orphanage was abuzz with excitement as the workmen arrived with their tools and supplies. At breakfast, George Müller thanked the Lord for the weather as well as for the food. "He is a faithful Father," he reminded the children, "especially for those who have no father."

The work began quickly as the men broke open the brick wall surrounding the boiler with their sledgehammers and pry bars. By noon, the workmen had found the part of the boiler that was leaking. "I think we can rivet a new plate on here and save the boiler," said the foreman. "But it'll take another day to rebuild that wall."

But that afternoon, the workmen came up with an idea. "We've been talking," said the lead repairman. "We'd rather work all night. These children need the heat, so we might as well keep going."

God had not only held off the cold weather, but he had truly given the workmen a "mind to work" until the job was completed. Not one child suffered from cold.

*Trust is knowing that God will take care
of your needs.*

FROM GOD'S WORD:

Give all your worries to him, because he cares about you (1 Peter 5:7).

LET'S TALK ABOUT IT:

1. Why did George Müller tell the children about this need before God answered his prayer?
2. What two things did Müller and the children pray for?
3. What is one thing you need that only God can give you?

MENNO SIMONS

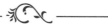

A Prophet of Peace

Menno Simons was born in the northern Netherlands in 1496. He was ordained a Catholic priest in 1524 and served until he became uncomfortable with some teachings of the Roman Catholic Church, such as baptizing infants.

Believing that the Bible was the Christian's highest authority, Menno Simons turned to the New Testament. From reading it, he came to believe that the state church was wrong about several important points. He left the priesthood in 1536 and was rebaptized by Obbe Philips.

People who were baptized a second time were often called Anabaptists, meaning rebaptizers. Menno was soon asked to become a preacher and leader among the congregations of Anabaptists in northwestern Europe. In time, his followers were called Mennonites.

Menno and most Anabaptists believed in peace and refused to use violence against anyone, even when they were in danger. However, even though the Anabaptists were not rebels against the state, their rejection of the idea of a state church seemed like a threat to both the Roman Church and the state. And both the Roman Church and the Holy Roman Empire tried to wipe them out. At times, this also happened under the Lutheran Church in Germany and in surrounding countries. And it occasionally happened where the Reformed Church was united with a state.

At first, persecution was severe for all reformers, but it was most deadly to the Anabaptists, who never wished to make an alliance with a state government. Four to twelve thousand Anabaptists in Europe were killed because of their faith.

In 1543, the Holy Roman Emperor offered a hundred gold coins to anyone who would betray Menno Simons. However, by God's grace and heroic help from other believers, Menno was never caught. He died a natural death in 1561.

INTEGRITY

An "Outlaw" for the Lord

 ven though he was a Roman Catholic priest in the Netherlands, Menno Simons had never read the Bible. But some of the state church's teachings didn't seem right, so he began to read the New Testament for himself.

As he began to teach directly from the Bible, some of his listeners began to think that the state church was false. "We need a new church, a true church," they said eagerly.

"No," said Menno, who enjoyed the life of a parish priest. "That's not necessary. Let's just wait. Things may change. We'll just keep on holding church services as usual even though we know some of these practices are false."

But other people who felt the state church was wrong were doing something about it. A group called the Münsterites were willing to fight to bring about change. "At least they are doing *something*!" people said. Frustrated, many of Menno Simons' own people joined the Münsterites in a nearby castle called The Old Cloister. Knowing that government troops might come and try to break them up, they got ready to protect themselves with swords and other weapons.

"Don't do this," warned Menno. "Turning to violence is one of the mistakes the state church has made. The Bible does not allow it. Don't forget what Jesus said, 'All who draw the sword will die by the sword.'"

But the people, most of whom couldn't read the Bible anyway, wouldn't listen because Menno was not living according to his own beliefs.

Then, on April 5, 1535, government soldiers stormed The Old Cloister and broke through its defenses. Of the 300 people inside, 130 were killed in battle. Afterward, most of the other rebels were executed.

Among those killed was Peter Simons, Menno's own brother. Menno had not been able to talk him out of joining the rebels. "Who are you to tell me what to do?" his brother had challenged. "You tell us that the Roman Church is false, but you won't do anything about it. You stay in it, enjoying the salary of a priest."

In the days that followed, Menno was very sad. "They made a mistake," he said, "but at least they had the courage to live by what they believed. I, on the other hand, cared for nothing but my own comfort and what people thought of me. Now look what has happened! These people were like sheep without a shepherd, and I refused—for selfish reasons—to become a shepherd to them. They may have been wrong, but their deaths are my fault."

Falling to his knees, he prayed, "Lord, give me a clean heart and forgive me for seeking the easy life. Give me the courage to follow you boldly, whatever the cost."

In January of 1536, he resigned as a priest and was soon baptized by Obbe Philips. For the rest of his life, he was an "outlaw" from the state but faithful to God.

*Integrity is living honestly according to
what you believe.*

FROM GOD'S WORD:

Jesus said to all of them, "If people want to follow
me, they must give up the things they want. They
must be willing to give up their lives daily to follow
me. Those who want to save their lives will give up
true life. But those who give up their lives for me
will have true life" (Luke 9:23–24).

LET'S TALK ABOUT IT:

1. What happened when Menno Simons began
   reading the Bible for himself?
2. Why wouldn't the people accept Menno's
   guidance when he warned them not to use
   weapons?
3. Safety and comfort are not the most important
   things in life. Describe a time when you risked
   one or the other to do what was right.

LOYALTY
Reward: 100 Gold Coins

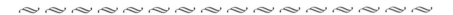

he city mayors and other government officials of the Netherlands were upset. They were unable to stop the underground Anabaptist churches from growing! One letter from the city of Leeuwarden to Emperor Charles V of the Holy Roman Empire complained, "We could have stamped out the Anabaptists if it weren't for a former priest, Menno Simons, who is one of the main leaders in this area. He goes everywhere making new followers."

The officials arrested and tortured many Anabaptists in order to destroy the new church. If the people cooperated with the officials by denying or rejecting their faith and giving out the names of other Anabaptists, they were executed quickly and "mercifully" by having their heads chopped off. If they would not deny their faith and refused to tell the names of any other Anabaptists, they suffered the slower, more painful death of being burned at the stake.

But no matter how cruel the government was, the underground church continued to grow.

"This is not working," complained the emperor to his agents.

"We need to capture this Menno Simons. Any time you catch an Anabaptist, focus on only one thing: Find out where Menno Simons is hiding!"

So the officials tried. After much torture, Tjard Reynders admitted that he had let Menno Simons stay in his house once and had even been baptized by him, but he would not deny his faith. Another man, Sjouck Hayes of the city of Leeuwarden, finally confessed that he had once heard Menno Simons preach in a field outside the city.

But the government was no closer to catching Menno. "We're going about this all wrong," said the emperor. "Why should the people help us catch Menno if we kill them as soon as they admit to being Anabaptists? What we need is to find someone we can bribe. Let's offer a full pardon to anyone who helps us. Better yet, let's offer a hundred gold coins and a pardon. If there is no danger to the person who helps us, we should be able to find someone to tell us where he is."

So the emperor sent out the notice to all the officials in the Netherlands, where Menno Simons was known to travel and preach. This reward notice was printed and posted and read aloud in the city squares.

The government's efforts to catch Menno Simons made life hard for him. He was always on the run. Once he wrote, "In all these countries, I cannot find a cabin or hut where my poor wife and our little children can be safe for very long. Sooner or later we must pack up and run." He often traveled by himself at night and would sneak into a town, preach once or twice, and be gone before the authorities heard that he had been there.

During the next couple of years, many people were baptized by Menno, and the new church grew quickly. Government agents captured and tortured several new Christians and put them to death—but no one betrayed the traveling preacher known as Menno Simons.

Loyalty is remaining true to your friends
no matter what.

FROM GOD'S WORD:
Many people claim to be loyal, but it is hard to find a trustworthy person (Proverbs 20:6).

LET'S TALK ABOUT IT:
1. Why did Menno Simons' family have to move so often?
2. How did the emperor finally think he would catch Menno? Why didn't it work?
3. In the Bible, being faithful often means the same thing as being loyal. God wants us to be faithful or loyal to Him. How do people sometimes betray God?

SACRIFICIAL LOVE
The Ship in the Ice

enno Simons and his son Jan were walking along the docks of Wismar's icy harbor. "Look," said Jan, "there's a light in the harbor. No ship would sail now, would it, Father?"

"I don't think so," said Menno Simons. It was December 1553, and the coldest weather he had ever seen in northern Germany. "No ship has left Wismar for a week."

"Maybe a ship is trying to come into port then."

"If so, it will take the city rescue crew to save them in this weather," said the preacher.

"Now, that's a job I'd like!" grinned Jan.

Simons shook his head. "It might be exciting, but it's also dangerous. We'll see what happens by morning."

The next day when father and son passed the same way, no one had rescued the people from the frozen ship. After asking a few questions, they discovered why.

"Those are John Laski's people out there," growled a city official standing with other onlookers on the icy dock. "They're part of the Reformed Church, and Germany is Lutheran now. Emperor Charles V chased them to England seven years ago. Ha! Now Queen Mary has ruled that England is Catholic again, so they want to return. But we Lutherans don't want them! We already have too much trouble from the Mennonites."

Menno Simons' face got very grim. He grabbed his son's arm and hurried down the street.

Within an hour, several of the leading members of the underground Anabaptist church of Wismar gathered in Menno's home. Jan and his sisters listened to them talk.

"Why should we do anything?" asked one man. "It's not our concern that they're trapped on that ship. Menno, don't forget that John Laski chased you out of East Friesland. He killed and badly treated many of our people there. And that was after pretending to be friendly to you!"

"But now they need help," said Gertrude, Menno's wife. "If the city crew won't rescue them, we must."

"If we go out there, everyone in town will know about it, and we will be in worse trouble," objected another Mennonite. "Besides, it's *extremely* dangerous out on that ice. And we don't have the training or the equipment."

"There are children on that ship," Menno argued. "We must help them. I understand Laski's own children may be out there."

"All the more reason to leave them there," grumbled a serious voice. "Whether Reformed, Roman Catholic, or Lutheran—everyone is against us. Why should we help them?"

"Brothers and sisters," pleaded Menno, "what would Jesus do?" His words silenced the protests, and in a few minutes all agreed to take food out to the ship and offer the refugees safety from the storm.

The Reformed Church refugees were rescued and seemed thankful. But, hoping to make friends with the Lutherans, some refugees gave to the city officials a list of the Mennonites who had helped them. Within less than a year, the Mennonites were chased from the city.

Sacrificial love sometimes means returning good for evil.

FROM GOD'S WORD:
"But I say to you who are listening, love your enemies. Do good to those who hate you, bless those who curse you, pray for those who are cruel to you" (Luke 6:27–28).

LET'S TALK ABOUT IT:
1. Why were the Reformed Church people returning to the Netherlands?
2. Why didn't the Wismar city officials want them to come ashore in their land?
3. Sometimes even when you do something kind to someone, that person is not kind back to you. Describe a time when something like this happened to you. How did it make you feel? What do you think Jesus wants you to do in the future?

MARY SLESSOR

—————— ⚜ ——————

Pioneer Missionary to Calabar

Mary Slessor was born in Aberdeen, Scotland, in 1848, the daughter of a shoemaker. When David Livingstone, famous missionary and African explorer, died in 1874, his life inspired many to become missionaries—including this red-haired Scottish lassie. Two years later, Mary arrived in Calabar (what we know today as southern Nigeria, Africa). She was twenty-seven.

Mary's first assignment was to a mission station along the coast. Uncomfortable with the difference in how the European missionaries and African people lived, Mary chose to live simply, African-style. This made it possible for her to send the money she earned back to Scotland to support her family.

But Mary, like David Livingstone, was a pioneer, and she wanted to travel deep into Africa. She wanted to help the Okoyong people, who had never heard the Gospel.

When she arrived, the only trade was in "guns, gin, and chains," but Mary encouraged the people to grow more crops to sell—both so they could live better and to give them less time for drinking and fighting.

Mary also believed that "school and the Gospel" went hand in hand. People had to learn to read so they could read the Bible for themselves. She also challenged customs and ways that went against the teachings of the Bible, such as witchcraft, twin murder, human sacrifice, polygamy, and slavery. Her fame as a peacemaker soon brought chiefs from other villages to seek her advice. In 1892, the British appointed her as official vice-consul (similar to a judge) for the area.

In 1902, after fifteen years among the Okoyong people, eleven young people were baptized, seven of whom were her own adopted children. But Mary was restless. There were still tribes who had never heard the Gospel of Jesus Christ! She was due to go to Scotland on furlough in 1904—instead, Mary spent her own time and money to search out a new mission base in order to reach the fierce Aros and Ibibios tribes.

Finally, on January 13, 1915, at the age of sixty-six, she became sick with a fever and dysentery for the last time. But her spirit and influence lived on.

COURAGE
The Bully's Challenge

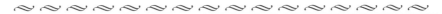

The bouncing mane of red hair was all that showed of Mary Slessor as she walked through the narrow streets of Dundee, Scotland, surrounded by a noisy, laughing crowd of boys and girls. The factory girl had been up early, knocking on slum doors and waking the sleepy children. Now they were on their way to Sunday school at Wishart Church.

But as they turned a corner, their way was blocked by a gang of bullies. "We don't want you here," snarled the biggest boy, clearly the leader. "Go on—get out."

Frightened, the boys and girls scattered. But twenty-year-old Mary Slessor stood right where she was.

"No, I won't," she said. "I'm going to teach Sunday school today. Why don't you come with us?"

The bully's eyes narrowed. "I'll make you leave!" he threatened. As he spoke he pulled a cord from his pocket with a heavy lead weight tied on the end. When Mary didn't move, he began to swing the cord slowly around his head. Still Mary didn't budge. Several of the children with her screamed as the lead weight came swinging closer and closer to Mary's head. On the next slow swing, the weight grazed her forehead, but Mary didn't flinch.

Amazed at her courage, the bully stopped swinging. "The lassie's game, boys!" he said with respect and admiration, stepping aside. As Mary once more gathered the younger boys and girls and went down the steps into the basement Sunday school room, the bigger boys all trooped after her.

Many years later when Mary Slessor was a missionary living in a mud house along the Calabar River in West Africa, she received a package from Scotland. With a smile, she unwrapped a framed picture of a handsome man with a pretty wife and several small children. "Who is it, Mama?" asked Janie, her adopted African daughter, as she looked at the picture.

So Mary told Janie and her other adopted children about the bully who had come to Sunday school. He was now grown up and had a good job.

"Look!" cried Janie. "Something's written on the back!"

It said: "To Mary Slessor, in grateful remembrance of the day that was the turning point of my life."

Courage is standing up for what's right even when it means danger.

FROM GOD'S WORD:
So my dear brothers and sisters, stand strong. Do not let anything change you. Always give yourselves fully to the work of the Lord, because you know that your work in the Lord is never wasted (1 Corinthians 15:58).

LET'S TALK ABOUT IT:

1. What do you think would have happened if Mary Slessor had run away from the bully that day?
2. In what way was Mary already being a missionary when she spoke to the bully?
3. Discuss how a Christian might decide when it is time to be courageous and "stand firm."

MERCY
"Run, Ma! Run!"

~~~~~~~~~~~~~~~~~~~~~~~~~~~~~~~

ary Slessor sat on the porch of her bamboo and mud house rocking a small child. Several other Okoyong children played around her feet. They had been brought to her either because they were sick, or orphans, or unwanted. The mission house in the village of Ekenge had become well known as a house of safety and refuge.

Just then a boy from the village came flying down the path and into the fenced yard. "Run, Ma! Run!" he yelled, pointing into the jungle.

Immediately Mary placed the child in the arms of a helper and ran after the boy. She knew what his cry meant: twins had been born in a nearby village, and if she did not get there in time, they might be killed.

The Okoyong people were deathly afraid of the "twin curse." When twins were born, they thought that one of the babies must have been fathered by the devil. Since they didn't know which one, both twins were usually left in the jungle to die, and the mother was sent away in shame.

As she ran barefoot and bareheaded through the jungle, Mary

came upon a loud, angry group of people. At the head of the line staggered a weeping woman, her clothes torn, carrying a wooden box on her head. People were spitting on her and shouting insults.

"Iye!" gasped Mary. Iye was a pretty slave woman who had been well liked by her mistress. Mary took the box and nearly cried out in horror. Two newborn babies had been stuffed in the bottom of the box under Iye's pots and pans. But one baby was still alive!

Mary quickly led the way back to her house. But when the group came close to her village, she stopped. If she took the "cursed" twin mother and her babies down the market road, she knew no one in the village would ever use the road again. And it was hard to make a good road in this part of the jungle. How could she show kindness to the twins' mother *and* the village people—even though she thought they were wrong? Quickly she asked some of the village men to cut a simple path through the vines and bushes directly to her house.

When Iye was safely in Mary's house, Mary sadly gave the dead twin a simple, Christian burial in her yard. The other twin, whom she named Susie, was rarely out of her arms. Curious villagers came to see the "monster" twin that "white Ma" had dared to rescue. But all they saw was a beautiful, happy child thriving with care and affection.

After a few days, Iye's mistress sent word that she was willing to have Iye back if she came without the child. Iye, who had been moaning about what had happened, was only too willing to leave her shame behind.

Soon baby Susie became queen of Mary's household. Even the villagers grew to like her. But when she started to walk, Susie pulled a pot of boiling water over and burned herself badly. As the child hung between life and death, none of the villagers went to their fields or to market. And when Susie went home to heaven on a Sunday morning, the whole village mourned with Mary Slessor. Even Iye came and cried at her child's grave. The "cursed twin" had become a blessing to all who knew her.

Mercy includes acts of kindness toward both the innocent and the guilty.

FROM GOD'S WORD:
Those who show mercy to others are happy, because God will show mercy to them (Matthew 5:7).

LET'S TALK ABOUT IT:
1. Why did the Okoyong people think having twins was a curse?
2. How did Mary Slessor show mercy toward the villagers, even though she knew they were wrong about the "twin curse"?
3. What do you think Jesus meant when He said, "Those who give mercy to others are blessed. Mercy will be given to them"?

PEACEMAKER
Standing in the Way

~~~~~~~~~~~~~~~~~~~~~~~~~~~~

he mission house in the village of Ekenge was getting crowded. Abused wives, abandoned children, and runaway slaves found refuge and safety there.

"Will you and your people help me build a new house?" Mary Slessor asked her friend Chief Edem.

"Sure, Ma, sure. We will be glad to help," said the chief, tipping his chair back against the side of his hut and puffing on his pipe.

But when several days passed and no one showed up to help, Mary took a big knife called a machete and began to clear the ground herself on the edge of the village.

As the people passed by, they shook their heads. Why was Ma in such a hurry? There was always tomorrow.

This was a difference between European and African culture that was hard for Mary Slessor to get used to. She was a doer. The Okoyong people, on the other hand, never seemed to be in a hurry, *except . . .*

Except when a fight was brewing.

One day as Mary was plastering the walls of the new mission

house with mud, she heard the sound of running feet. Then there was a loud commotion in the village, followed by much shouting and more running feet.

Worried, Mary washed the mud off her hands and hurried into the village. But all the men were gone!

"Some robbers stole two slave women and two slave men from Ma Eme's farm," a young boy said excitedly. Ma Eme was the chief's sister. "Now they've gone to get justice."

"Were they drinking?" Mary asked.

The boy nodded.

Now Mary was really worried. The Okoyong idea of justice usually meant taking revenge on whoever had wronged them. They killed, tortured, burned houses or crops, or took slaves until their revenge was satisfied. And drinking only made it worse.

Running into the forest, she finally caught up with Chief Edem and his warriors, who had found the robbers in a nearby village. But the robbers were also armed with machetes and spears, so all that had happened so far was a lot of yelling and angry threats.

Mary marched into the space between the enemies. "Fighting and killing is the wrong way to solve problems," she said firmly. "Both sides must sit down and *palaver* [talk]. Then we will decide what to do."

The warriors from Ekenge were angry. But they couldn't kill the robbers with Ma Slessor standing in the way. Frustrated, they opened a cask of gin. Soon everyone was roaring drunk. This made it almost impossible to talk to the two sides, but Mary was determined. All day and all night she stood between them, trying to keep everyone calm.

Finally, she managed to get Chief Edem and the head robber to sit down and talk. She made the robbers agree to give back the stolen slaves and pay Ma Eme several baskets of seed for the trouble they'd caused. Then she made Chief Edem agree that there would be no killing or getting even.

As dawn brought the new day, Mary wearily walked home with Chief Edem, the rescued slaves, and the warriors with hangovers. She knew it was hard for the people to give up the old ways, even when she taught them what the Bible said. Slavery and drunkenness were still big problems among the people. But she was grateful. At least today, precious lives had been saved.

A peacemaker is someone who brings enemies together with a peaceful solution.

FROM GOD'S WORD:

So let us try to do what makes peace and helps one another (Romans 14:19).

LET'S TALK ABOUT IT:

1. Why do you think Mary Slessor took the risk of putting herself between the two groups of enemies?
2. In what way was the agreement they reached good for both sides?
3. What are some ways you could be a peacemaker at home? at school? on the job?

HUDSON TAYLOR

Englishman With a Pigtail

James Hudson Taylor was born in 1832 in Yorkshire, England. While preparing in college to be a medical missionary, he also studied the Mandarin Chinese language. On September 19, 1853, he set sail for China on the clipper ship *Dumfries*, a missionary for the Chinese Evangelization Society.

Unlike many other Englishmen, Taylor respected Chinese ways and customs, except when they went against the teaching of the Bible. To show his respect for the Chinese, he wore Chinese clothes and even grew his hair into a long pigtail. Other missionaries disapproved. But one English woman who admired Hudson's courage in dressing like the Chinese was Maria Dyer. She and Hudson Taylor were happily married on January 20, 1858.

Hudson Taylor was unusual in another way. He thought that Christians should not get into debt. He also believed Christian workers should pray to God about their needs rather than asking people for money.

Because of these differences, Taylor left the Chinese Evangelization Society and continued mission work on his own. God not only provided all his physical needs, but his ministry among the Chinese people helped many to become Christians.

However, in 1860, while director of the London Mission Hospital in Ningpo, China, Taylor became so ill that he and Maria had to return to England. Here he translated the New Testament into the Ningpo Chinese dialect. He also founded the China Inland Mission and found new missionaries to go inland instead of just to the cities on the coast. He and his team returned to China in 1866.

Under Hudson Taylor's leadership, the mission grew and spread throughout all of China. When he retired in 1901, eight hundred missionaries served with the China Inland Mission. Also, for the first time, these missionaries from several church denominations were working together to spread the Good News.

Hudson Taylor died in Changsha in 1905.

FAITH
The Fastest Boat Home

"What do you want?" Hudson Taylor whispered to the dark figure who was creeping up on him in the night.

It was well after midnight, and he was exhausted. That morning, while traveling in the interior of China, he had discovered that his servant had stolen all his luggage—almost everything he owned—and left him alone in a strange and dangerous city. Finally, he gave up searching for his unfaithful servant and lay down on the stone steps of a Buddhist temple, his small purse under his head. He would have fallen asleep if he had not noticed the man creeping up on him.

At Taylor's whispered question, the man left without answering. Relieved, Taylor turned over and had just managed to doze off when he awoke to find two more people sneaking up on him. He remained very still and prayed that God would protect him. They came closer and felt around, trying to find Taylor's money and other valuables.

When one of the thieves began to feel under Taylor's head, Taylor again said, "What do you want?"

"Oh—nothing," said the man, startled. "But you better go to

sleep or you won't be able to travel tomorrow. We'll sit here and protect you. Don't be afraid."

"I don't want your 'protection,'" said Taylor. "I trust in my God. He will take care of me."

One of the men left and came back with a third man, but when Hudson Taylor began to pray out loud and sing, they finally gave up and went away.

The next morning, Taylor thanked God for protecting him. He also realized that he had been so upset the night before about losing all his belongings, that he hadn't asked God for a safe place to sleep.

Taylor felt ashamed. If he had prayed, God might have given him a better place to sleep.

As he started the long trip home, he asked God to forgive him for not having more faith. He also prayed that God would help him be more concerned about telling people the Gospel than about losing his things. His prayer made him feel so much better that his day's walk did not seem long or hard. That night, in answer to his prayer, a stranger took him in.

The next day, the stranger arranged for a mail boat to take Taylor down the canal to Shanghai. "He has been robbed," announced his new friend to the boatmen, "but he will pay you when he gets home. And if he doesn't, I'll pay you when you return."

The mail boat was fast, and Hudson Taylor got back to Shanghai safely. He never did recover his luggage, but he realized God would take care of him anyway. A short while later, he received a letter in the mail—with exactly enough money to replace everything his servant had stolen from him.

Faith is the confidence that even in frightening times or places, God is still in control.

FROM GOD'S WORD:

My God will use his wonderful riches in Christ Jesus to give you everything you need (Philippians 4:19).

LET'S TALK ABOUT IT:

1. Why didn't Hudson Taylor pray and ask God to help him find a place to spend the night after his servant stole his luggage?
2. How did God provide for Taylor when he stopped worrying about his luggage?
3. Name one thing God has provided for you and thank Him for it.

TRUST
The Evil Plot

~~~~~~~~~~~~~~~~~~~~~~~~~~~~~~~~~~~~~~

Honorable teacher," said Hudson Taylor's Chinese assistant, wringing his hands, "there is going to be much trouble. I must tell you about it."

It was unusual for Taylor's faithful assistant to worry without a reason, so Taylor stopped studying and looked up.

"You have heard how the British are making war on the city of Canton. Their big guns have killed many, many people. That has made the Cantonese people living here in Ningpo very angry. They are planning to kill all the foreigners in revenge."

"How could they possibly do that?" asked Taylor. "We're scattered all over the city."

"They are waiting until Sunday evening. They know that all the missionaries and most of the foreign merchants gather together to worship in one of your homes. They plan to surround the house and kill everyone present."

"Don't worry," said Taylor, turning back to his studies. "The police would never allow such a thing."

"Not so!" said his assistant. "The mayor of the city has given his secret permission. The police will stay away."

Suddenly, Taylor became worried. He closed his book and looked his assistant in the eye. "How do you know this?"

"I have a friend who is Cantonese. He warned me to get away and save my own life."

"Maybe you better do that," said Taylor, finally taking the threat seriously. "Why don't you go visit your sister in the country this weekend."

"But, honorable teacher, what about you . . . and the others?"

"I'm not sure what we will do, but thank you for the warning."

Realizing the danger, Taylor called together several missionaries. Together they decided that if the mayor and the police wouldn't protect them, the only one they could turn to was God. So they began to pray.

At the very time that they were praying, a higher government official was meeting with the mayor, and he learned about the plot to kill the missionaries.

"That's a foolish idea," he said. "It will surely cause international problems."

"I will just say that I knew nothing about it until it happened." The mayor shrugged. "I will blame it on the Cantonese. If they get in trouble, then I will be free of two groups of outsiders, the English *and* the Cantonese."

"You would never get away with it," said the government official. "For one thing, I now know about the plot. You had better put a stop to it."

So the mayor sent word to the Cantonese warning them not to harm the missionaries.

When the missionaries later discovered that God was working to protect them at the very time they were praying, they rejoiced and praised God for His care.

Trust is believing that God can protect you.

FROM GOD'S WORD:
Let me hide under the shadow of your wings until the trouble has passed (Psalm 57:1b).

LET'S TALK ABOUT IT:
1. Why were the Cantonese planning to kill the missionaries?
2. How did God protect them?
3. Tell about a time when you were afraid that someone would hurt you. Did you ask God to protect you? What happened?

OBEDIENCE
"Why Didn't You Come Sooner?"

udson Taylor was discouraged. He had been preaching in the city of Ningpo for a year. The Chinese were polite and enjoyed gathering to hear Taylor speak. Discussing new ideas was fun to them. But no one seemed to take the Gospel seriously. No one believed it.

And then, after one message, when Taylor felt most like giving up, a respected man stood up and turned to his Chinese countrymen.

"I have been searching for the truth a long time," he said earnestly. "My father and my grandfathers before me searched for the truth, but they never found it. I have traveled far and wide looking for it. I have tried Confucianism, Taoism, and Buddhism, but have found no rest."

Taylor looked at the man with new interest. He knew that this man was a leading officer among the Ningpo Buddhists. What was he saying? Was he saying that his religion gave him no peace?

"But tonight," said the man honestly, "tonight I have found

rest. I have heard the truth, and from now on I am a believer in Jesus."

Hudson Taylor could hardly believe his ears. Could it be true?

A short time later, the man proved his sincerity by taking Hudson with him to the Buddhist meeting and giving his testimony. Soon one of the man's friends also became a Christian and was baptized.

However, a few nights after the man had accepted Jesus as his Savior, he asked Hudson Taylor a very hard question. "How long have the people in your land known about Jesus?"

"Oh, hundreds of years," answered Hudson Taylor.

"What?" said the man in amazement. "You knew the truth for hundreds of years and didn't come to tell us? My father searched for the truth all his life and died without finding it. *Why didn't you come sooner?*"

It was a hard question. Jesus had told His followers to go into all the world and preach the Gospel to everyone, but too often Christians don't obey Him. This man knew the result. He knew people who wanted to know the truth and were just waiting for someone to come and tell them.

Wanting to obey his newfound Savior, the former Buddhist leader spent the rest of his life telling others about Jesus.

Obedience is doing what God has asked you to do.

FROM GOD'S WORD:

Jesus said to his followers, "Go everywhere in the world, and tell the Good News to everyone" (Mark 16:15).

LET'S TALK ABOUT IT:

1. Why was Hudson Taylor discouraged?
2. What had the Buddhist man been looking for all his life?
3. Think of someone you know who does not know about Jesus. Pray that God will help you tell that person the Good News about Jesus.

HARRIET TUBMAN

Conductor on the Underground Railroad

Araminta Ross was born a slave around 1820 on a Maryland plantation owned by Edward Brodas. "Minty," as she was called, was taught Bible stories, gospel songs, and spirituals by her deeply religious parents. But in the tense years just before the Civil War, slaves were not allowed to gather in groups, not even for church.

The Brodas plantation was falling on hard times. Sometimes Edward Brodas "hired out" his slaves to make ends meet—including little Minty. But she got sent back home each time because people thought she was "stubborn" or "stupid." Deciding that Minty was hopeless at housework, Brodas put her to work in the fields, which was much harder—but also much more to her liking. By age eleven, she had shed the nickname Minty. Folks now called her Harriet, after her mother.

In 1844, at the age of twenty-four, Harriet married a free Negro named John Tubman. When she talked to her husband about running away, he said he would tell her master if she tried it! But Harriet couldn't give up the hope of freedom. She had heard about an "underground railroad" that took slaves to freedom in the northern states.

In 1849, she knew the time had come. She traveled only at night, using all her knowledge of the woods to make her way north. At each friendly "station" or stop on the way, she was told where to go next.

When she arrived in Pennsylvania, she was excited by her new freedom. But instead of sitting back and enjoying freedom for herself, Harriet went back to lead other slaves to freedom— over three hundred during her lifetime.

During the Civil War, she was recruited as a "nurse" and a spy for the Union Army. But even though she was greatly respected, she never received any of the army pay owed her.

After the war, when slavery finally ended, Harriet began a home for the sick, poor, and homeless in Auburn, New York. She died there in 1913 at the age of ninety-three.

COMPASSION
Blow to the Forehead

hirteen-year-old Harriet saw the silent, moody slave slip away from the cornhusking bee on the Brodas plantation even before the overseer did. But within minutes, she heard the overseer shout, "Hey! You, there—stop!"

But the slave didn't stop. He started to run, with the overseer fast on his heels. Not quite understanding why she did so, Harriet dropped the corn she was husking and followed. Something bad was going to happen. She had to do something. A slave who tried to run away and was caught was beaten severely—and then sold down South to a chain gang.

The runaway tried to hide in a little country store at the crossroads, but the overseer went in after him. The slave was cornered, breathing heavily, and the overseer threatened to whip him then and there.

"You, girl!" the angry overseer shouted at Harriet when she appeared in the doorway. "Help me tie this man up."

Harriet didn't move. Realizing she was giving him a chance, the slave darted past Harriet and started to run. In an effort to stop him, the overseer grabbed a two-pound weight and threw it at the runaway. But in that same moment, Harriet stepped in the way.

The weight struck her full in the forehead, knocking her backward. She was unconscious for days, then she slipped in and out of a stupor for months. But as Harriet slowly recovered, a constant prayer was on her lips—for her master: "Change his heart, Lord."

The wound finally healed, but for the rest of her life Harriet suffered terrible headaches and a strange "sleeping sickness" that made her suddenly black out for a few minutes or even a few hours.

As winter turned to spring, a rumor went around the slave quarters: The master was going to sell Harriet to the next slave trader who came along for her part in letting the slave escape. Angry, her prayer changed. "Lord, if you're never going to change Massa Brodas' heart—then kill him, Lord! Take him out of the way."

Within weeks, Edward Brodas became ill. He died even before the new tobacco crop had been planted. Horrified, Harriet thought she had killed him!

Edward Brodas had promised Harriet's parents that they would have their freedom when he died. But when his will was read, it said only that none of his slaves could be sold outside the state of Maryland.

Even when she heard this terrible news, Harriet felt sorry that her master had died without changing his heart. She often said, "I would give the world full of silver and gold to bring that poor soul back. . . . I would give myself. I would give everything!"

Compassion is bearing someone else's burden as if it were your own.

FROM GOD'S WORD:

By helping each other with your troubles, you truly obey the law of Christ (Galatians 6:2).

LET'S TALK ABOUT IT:

1. In what way did Harriet have compassion for the runaway slave? In what way did she have compassion for her master?
2. How is it possible to have compassion both for people who suffer and for people who cause the suffering?
3. What is the "law of Christ" that we fulfill when we help each other with troubles? (See Galatians 5:14.)

JOY
Liberty . . . or Death

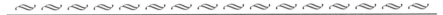

ohn," whispered Harriet to her new husband, "you already have your freedom, but I want to be free, too. Why don't we run away up north to one of the free states where—"

"That's foolishness!" interrupted John Tubman, a free black man who had asked her owner for permission to marry the twenty-four-year-old Harriet. He didn't want any trouble. "If I hear you talking that way again, I'll tell your master!"

Harriet was hurt. If John loved her, wouldn't he want her to be free, too? She never brought up the subject again—but she thought about it all the time.

She had heard about the Underground Railroad that took slaves to freedom in the northern states. "There is one of two things I have a right to," she told herself. "Liberty or death. If I cannot have one, I will have the other, for no man will take me alive. I will fight for my liberty as long as my strength lasts, and when the time comes for me to go, the Lord will let them take me."

One night, she silently made her way through the woods to the home of a white Quaker woman who had once told her, "If you ever need help, come to me." There she learned that the Underground Railroad was not a railroad at all, but a network of "stations"—farmers and townspeople who were willing to hide slaves and help them reach freedom.

Harriet traveled only at night. At each friendly station, she was told where to go next. Along the way, she traveled in a wagon under a load of vegetables, was rowed up the Choptank River by a man she had never seen before, was hidden in a haystack, spent a week in a potato hole in a cabin that belonged to a family of free blacks, was hidden in the attic of a Quaker family, and was befriended by German farmers.

Harriet's daily prayer became, "Lord, I'm going to hold steady on to you, and you've got to see me through." Still suffering from her head injury, she sometimes fell asleep right on the road, but somehow she managed to escape being discovered.

Near Wilmington, Delaware, Harriet had been told to hide in a graveyard. A man came wandering through muttering, "I have a ticket for the railroad." This man disguised Harriet in workman's clothes and took her to Thomas Garrett's house, a famous Quaker who worked hard to end slavery. Garrett, who had a shoe shop, gave her new shoes and fancy women's clothes and drove her in his buggy north of Wilmington. Then he gave Harriet, who couldn't read or write, a paper with the word PENNSYLVANIA written on it so she could recognize the sign when she crossed the state line.

Harriet finally crossed into Pennsylvania—a free state. She had traveled a total of ninety miles. In spite of her tiredness, joy flooded her from head to toe. She was free! The feeling was like nothing she'd ever felt before.

Harriet looked wonderingly at her hands to see if she was the same person. "There was such a glory over everything," she said later. "The sun came like gold through the trees, and over the fields, and I felt like I was in heaven."

Joy is a gift from God, a taste of what it will be like in heaven.

FROM GOD'S WORD:
Crying may last for a night, but joy comes in the morning (Psalm 30:5b).

LET'S TALK ABOUT IT:
1. Why do you think John Tubman didn't want to help his wife run away to freedom?
2. Try to imagine what Harriet felt like when she reached freedom. How would you describe it?
3. What kinds of experiences here on earth give us a taste of the joy waiting for us in heaven?

PERSEVERANCE
"Wanted: Dead or Alive!"

~~~~~~~~~~~~~~~~~~~~~~~~~~~~~~~~

"Shhh," Harriet Tubman hissed. The farmhouse in the clearing was dark. Where was the signal light that was supposed to welcome them?

Harriet had lost track of how many trips she'd made back to Maryland to rescue slaves. She had gone back the first few times to lead members of her own family to freedom. Then she kept going back—taking any slave willing to risk the hard road to freedom. But it was dangerous. Posters with Harriet's name and picture were posted all over Maryland: "Wanted: Harriet Tubman—dead or alive! Reward $40,000." The runaways had to sleep in the woods during the day and travel only at night.

Tonight the runaway slaves (Harriet called them her passengers) were exhausted and hungry. Their feet dragged slower and slower. Now they had reached the next station on the Underground Railroad. Creeping closer, Harriet knocked at the farmhouse door.

The door opened a crack. "Who is it?" whispered a frightened voice.

Harriet gave the password: "A friend with friends."

"The slave-catchers searched my house yesterday," said the frightened voice. "Go away! Quickly!" And the door slammed shut.

The runaway slaves were dismayed. They were so tired, so hungry . . . how could they keep going?

But they had to keep going. They stumbled back into the woods. Hunger gnawed at their bellies. Their feet were bruised. When the sun started to come up, they crawled under the bushes and leaves and fell into an uneasy sleep.

But Harriet couldn't sleep. She knew the runaways were too tired to go much farther. They needed a friend, someone to help them. Over and over she prayed to her heavenly Friend: "Lord, I'm going to hold steady on to you, and you've got to see us through."

As night fell once more, she heard a voice. Someone was coming! The others shrank back under the bushes, fear in their eyes. Then they heard a man's voice mumbling to himself, "My wagon stands in the barnyard across the way. The horse is in the stable. The harness hangs on a nail." Still mumbling, the man kept walking and was soon gone.

Harriet closed her eyes in relief. God *had* sent a friend to help them!

When it was dark, Harriet crept by herself to the edge of the woods. Sure enough, there was a wagon standing in a barnyard. In the barn was a sturdy horse. And in the wagon were a stack of blankets and baskets of food.

Quickly harnessing the horse, Harriet drove the wagon back to get her passengers.

"Praise God! Thank you, Jesus!" they cried as they crawled into the wagon. Harriet slapped the reins on the horse's rump. They were back on the road to freedom!

Harriet kept going South, leading more than 300 slaves to freedom. At the end of her life, she said, "On my Underground Railroad, I never ran my train off the track, and I never lost a passenger."

Perseverance is continuing to do what is right,
even when you get tired or run into problems.

FROM GOD'S WORD:

We must not become tired of doing good. We will receive our harvest of eternal life at the right time if we do not give up (Galatians 6:9).

LET'S TALK ABOUT IT:

1. Why do you think Harriet risked going back to help others once she had reached freedom?
2. What did Harriet do when she felt too tired to go on?
3. Do you sometimes get tired of doing good? (Talk about it.) What can you do to "persevere"?

WILLIAM TYNDALE

The Man Who Gave Us the English Bible

William Tyndale was born in England in the early 1490s. When he was a student at Cambridge University in the early 1520s, "Lutheran ideas" were a hot subject, so Tyndale probably formed many of his Protestant beliefs at this time.

After leaving the university, Tyndale joined the household of Sir John Walsh at Little Sodbury Manor in Gloucestershire, apparently as a tutor for the two Walsh boys. The Walshes were well known for taking in both nobility and clergy as guests, and Tyndale took part in many talks about theology (the study of God) around their table. He was shocked that even the people who served the church barely knew the Bible. He decided then and there that he was going to translate the Bible into English so that English-speaking people could read God's Word for themselves.

At that time, it was illegal to translate the Scriptures into English without official approval. (Churches used the Latin Vulgate, which the common people didn't understand.) Unable to get permission to go ahead with his project, Tyndale left England to do his translation work in Europe.

In 1526, the first complete English New Testament came off the printing press in Worms, Germany. Anne Boleyn was given a copy and showed it to King Henry VIII. But Henry rejected it, saying there was no need for an English Bible at that time. If and when one was done, he said, it should be done by respected scholars within the church, not by a priest who had skipped the country.

In 1535, Tyndale was betrayed while staying at the home of a kind merchant in Antwerp, Belgium. But even while Tyndale sat in prison, a fellow Oxford scholar, Miles Coverdale, finished an English translation of the Bible, mostly based on Tyndale's work. Only months after Tyndale was burned at the stake, King Henry put his stamp of approval on the Bible, and by 1539 every parish church was required to make copies available to its people.

VISION
The "Plow-Boy Challenge"

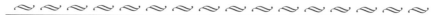

ut, Master Tyndale, *why* do we have to study these stuffy old Latin verbs?" the little boy complained.

William Tyndale hid a smile. "Because you must learn Latin in order to read the Scriptures," he said seriously.

"Then why don't they write the Bible in English?" his pupil grumbled.

"Hush!" said his older brother. "It's against the law!"

But the boy is right, Tyndale thought to himself. *Every man, woman, and child in England, whether rich or poor, should be able to read God's Word in English—not just hear it read in Latin, which most of them can't understand.* Just then the noise of clumping hooves and rattling wheels could be heard coming up the drive. Guests must be arriving for the noontime meal at Little Sodbury Manor.

William Tyndale had been at Little Sodbury only a short while as tutor for the two sons of Sir John and Lady Anne Walsh. Sir John and Lady Anne were well known for their hospitality, and all sorts of important nobles, ladies, and high-ranking clergy (people who worked for the church) were often gathered around their table. Tyndale enjoyed these meals; the conversations about politics or theology were always lively.

As it turned out, the talk around the Walshes' table that noon was even more lively than usual. Tyndale listened carefully as the guests argued.

"I hear the pope has said no to King Henry's request to divorce Queen Catherine. Poor fellow may not get a male heir after all."

" 'Poor fellow,' indeed! It's not the queen's fault that she has given birth to girls. Let Henry pass the crown to the princess!"

"Rubbish. King Henry will get his son—even if he has to leave the Catholic Church to do it!"

An abbot of the church, dressed in fine clothing and wearing a heavy gold necklace, turned to Tyndale. "Master Tyndale," he said, "I hear you picked up some 'reform' ideas at Cambridge College. What do you think?"

All eyes turned to the young scholar.

"It's not what I think," Tyndale said quietly. "It's what the Scriptures say. Tell me, Abbot, what the Bible says about divorce."

"Well, I . . . I . . . it's up to the pope," the abbot blustered. "The pope says—"

"We know what the pope says. What do the Scriptures say?"

The abbot grew red. "I will not have a country priest question me!" he thundered.

Tyndale was angry. "That's because you don't read the Bible—and the people can't because the only Bibles we have are written in Latin. We need an English version that can be read by king and common person alike."

The two Walsh boys looked at each other wide-eyed. What was Master Tyndale saying? Didn't he know it was against the law?

William Tyndale pointed a finger at the abbot. "If God spares my life, before many years pass I will help the boy behind the plow to know more of the Scriptures than you do!"

Vision is seeing beyond "the way things are"
to what needs to be done.

FROM GOD'S WORD:
Where there is no vision, the people perish.
(Proverbs 29:18a, KJV).

LET'S TALK ABOUT IT:
1. Why do you think the priests didn't want the Bible to be printed in a language the common people could read for themselves?
2. How do you think William Tyndale was going to help the "boy behind the plow" know more about the Scriptures than the priests?
3. Thank God that you have a Bible to read in your own language. Do you have an "extra" Bible at your house you could give to someone who doesn't have one?

PATIENCE
Burn the Books!

~~~~~~~~~~~~~~~~~~~~~~~~~~~~

The archbishop of Canterbury looked up from his desk. "Well, what is it?" he said to his secretary.

The secretary placed two leather-bound books on the archbishop's desk. "We have found two more copies of William Tyndale's English New Testament—from two different towns."

"What? I thought we ordered the booksellers not to sell these illegal books!" the archbishop said.

"But everyone is buying them. The booksellers are making good money," admitted the secretary.

The archbishop grabbed one of the books and opened it. "See here! He translated this word as 'repentance,' not 'penance.' If the people don't pay penance for their sins, the church will soon go broke. We must stop this right away!"

The archbishop paced back and forth behind his desk. "Obviously, our raids on the merchant ships have not stopped the shipment of these books into England . . . and as long as the booksellers are making money, they will sell them behind our backs." Suddenly the archbishop stopped pacing and a sly smile lit up his puffy face. "I know! We will buy up these New Testaments our-selves—all of them! Then we will destroy them. That will keep them out of the hands of the common people!"

It seemed like a good plan. The archbishop's men, acting like ordinary customers, visited all the booksellers and bought copies of Tyndale's New Testament. They did not threaten the booksellers because they wanted the booksellers to sell them as many copies as possible.

When the archbishop's men could find no more copies of the English New Testament, the archbishop ordered a big bonfire to be built. When the flames were roaring, his men threw all the books onto the fire.

"We've outsmarted that Tyndale now!" the archbishop laughed gleefully.

———

In Germany, Humphrey Monmouth, one of the shipping mer-chants who helped smuggle William Tyndale's New Testaments into England, told his friend about the archbishop's bonfire.

William Tyndale nodded thoughtfully. "Well, we still have the printing plates," he sighed. "I guess we have to start all over again—but it will take a while to raise the money for another printing."

A big grin spread over Humphrey Monmouth's face—and then he threw back his head and laughed out loud. Tyndale looked surprised; then his mouth dropped open as the stout mer-chant drew a leather bag of coins from his coat . . . then another, and another, and another.

"What's this?" Tyndale cried.

"Ha, ha—ho, ho," laughed Monmouth. "This is your share of the money from all the books that the archbishop bought—

enough for an even larger printing!"

William Tyndale laughed, too. "No one can stop God—not even the archbishop!"

Patience is knowing that, in the long run,
God's work will be done, in spite of
obstacles and setbacks.

FROM GOD'S WORD:

We have around us many people whose lives tell us what faith means. So let us run the race that is before us and never give up. We should remove from our lives anything that would get in the way and the sin that so easily holds us back (Hebrews 12:1).

LET'S TALK ABOUT IT:

1. Why was William Tyndale going to print more English New Testaments, even after the archbishop burned most of the copies from the first printing?
2. How did the archbishop's plan backfire?
3. When you try to do something good for God and it doesn't seem to work, why is it important to have patience?

FAITH
The False Friend

∼∼∼∼∼∼∼∼∼∼∼∼∼∼∼∼∼∼∼∼∼∼∼

What's the news from the king?" William Tyndale asked his host eagerly. "Did King Henry see my New Testament?"

Thomas Poyntz, an English merchant who had just returned to his home in Antwerp, Belgium, shook his head. "The news isn't good, my friend. The king rejected your English New Testament. He said it 'wasn't needed.' Not only that, but the hunt to find you has spread all over Europe. You must be very, very careful."

William Tyndale nodded. "I'm sure I will be safe here—thanks to your kindness. There are many foreigners in Antwerp. No one will notice me—especially since I spend most of my time in your attic working on my translation of the Old Testament."

As the two men said good-night, Tyndale added, "Oh, I almost forgot. Our young friend from the university, Henry Phillips, is coming for lunch next week. Will you be here?"

Thomas Poyntz frowned. "Unfortunately, no. I have another trip next week. But . . . I wish you would not see anyone while I am gone. It is too dangerous."

Tyndale patted his friend on the arm. "Come, come. Surely you are not worried about young Henry. He's very charming. He seems interested in our reform ideas."

"Too charming," worried Poyntz. "To me he rings as false as a counterfeit coin."

The next week, Henry Phillips knocked on the door of the Poyntz home. "Is Thomas here?" asked the handsome young man when William Tyndale answered the door.

"No, he is out of town," said Tyndale. "But we can still have lunch together."

"Say, I have an idea," said Phillips. "Why don't we go into the town for lunch. I have an errand to do on the way—that is, if you don't mind."

"Not at all," said Tyndale. "Let me get my cloak and hat."

As the two men walked the cobblestone streets, they came to a narrow alley, wide enough for only one person at a time. Phillips politely motioned for Tyndale to go ahead. As Tyndale came to the end of the alley, he was surprised to see two soldiers waiting at the other end. He started to turn back, but he saw Henry Phillips pointing at him. "This is the man—arrest him!" the young man cried.

William Tyndale had been betrayed!

For almost a year and a half, Tyndale sat in Antwerp's Vilvoord Prison, while Thomas Poyntz made many efforts to get him released. But in August 1536, William Tyndale was condemned as a heretic (someone who teaches something that goes against what a church believes)—to be strangled and burned at the stake.

As his sad friends gathered in October to see his heroic end, Tyndale lifted his face up to God and cried out, "O God! Open the King of England's eyes!"

Less than a year later, Thomas Poyntz received amazing news

from England. A man named Miles Coverdale had published the first ever complete Bible in English—largely based on William Tyndale's work—and King Henry VIII had given it his stamp of approval! Not only that, but by 1539, every parish church in England was required to make copies available to its people.

William Tyndale's prayer of faith had been answered!

Faith is the ability to leave unfinished work in God's hands.

FROM GOD'S WORD:

Faith means being sure of the things we hope for and knowing that something is real even if we do not see it (Hebrews 11:1).

LET'S TALK ABOUT IT:

1. What did William Tyndale mean when he prayed, "Open the King of England's eyes"?
2. Even though Tyndale died before his work on the English Bible was finished, how did God answer his prayer?
3. Are you feeling discouraged about something that seems unfinished that you can't do yourself? Together as a family, pray a prayer of faith, leaving it in God's hands.

JOHN WESLEY

The Founder of Methodism

John Wesley was the fifteenth child born to Samuel and Susanna Wesley in 1703 in Epworth, England. Another brother, Charles, was born two years later. Together, John and Charles Wesley made a difference in the world that is still felt today.

At Oxford College, Charles and John formed a group of students who wanted to study the Bible and worship together. They were very disciplined about their "religious duties." The young men also visited prisoners, paying their debts so they could be freed. "The Holy Club," as it was scornfully called by other students, was the beginning of the movement later known as the Methodists.

Ordained a minister, John rode from village to village preaching his high standards to people he assumed were already Christians. But in 1735, John became excited about going to America to preach to the Indians. Charles went, too, but both returned to England three years later, feeling that their time in America had been a failure.

John struggled with the fact that his strict religious disciplines did not make him sure of the salvation he desired. On May 24,

1738, he attended a meeting in Aldersgate Street, where someone read Luther's "Preface to the Epistle to the Romans," describing the change that God works in the heart through faith in Christ. As he listened, John felt his heart warm. "I felt I did trust in Christ, Christ alone for my salvation."

From that time on, John Wesley traveled all over England, Scotland, and Wales preaching a Gospel of faith and forming Methodist Societies to encourage Christians. His brother Charles wrote hundreds of hymns, earning Methodism the nickname, "the singing religion."

The Wesleys never intended to begin a new church, but they were prevented from preaching in the official state churches. So they preached anywhere and to anyone.

When an official demanded to know what was his parish, John replied, "The world is my parish." And so it was until his death at age eighty-eight in 1791.

DISCIPLINE
The Holy Club

~~~~~~~~~~~~~~~~~~~~~~~~~~~~~~~~~~~~~~~

ohn Wesley was discouraged. He had been ordained a minister at Oxford University and had been preaching for two years in the little village of Wroote. Why did the people seem so bored with religion? They were all Christians, weren't they? At least they came to church each Sunday. But he felt like he was preaching to the wall.

John was glad when Oxford called him back to teach. Maybe he wasn't cut out to be a parish minister after all. Besides, it would be great to see his younger brother Charles, who was still at Oxford.

"John!" Charles said when he returned. "There's a group of fellows I want you to meet. We've been meeting together Sunday evenings to study the Bible and pray."

Curious, John attended the meeting with his brother. The small group of students was talking about the spiritual "disciplines" they felt were needed to live a holy life: getting up at 4:00 A.M. for personal prayer and Bible reading, meeting together for Bible study and discussion, attending communion every week, regular fasting, and other rules. The group also agreed that serving other people was a religious duty. They decided to live on very little money and give the rest to pay the debts of prisoners and provide food and clothing to the needy.

"This is just the kind of group I like!" John thought. Growing up in a Christian home that was very poor, John was used to planning his day around Bible reading and prayer, and he wasn't used to luxuries. In fact, he was sure that a simple diet of bread, vegetables, and water was actually best for a healthy body. Because he was a few years older than the others and already a minister, he was soon recognized as the leader of the group.

Some of the other Oxford students laughed. "A bunch of Bible bigots!" they scoffed. "Always talking about the Bible."

"A group of *methodists*, you mean," said another. "They have a method for study, a method for eating, a method for religion, a method for charity . . . what's next?"

"It's The Holy Club," another joked. And the name stuck.

Some of the professors and university officials thought The Holy Club was a little *too* enthusiastic about religion. They tried to think of a way to stop it. But there was no stopping John and Charles Wesley, George Whitefield, and the others.

Years later, John Wesley would realize that the spiritual disciplines that were so important to him didn't *in themselves* bring salvation. Only accepting the gift of forgiveness for our sins through Jesus' death on the cross could do that. But it was here in The Holy Club that the movement that would become known as the Methodists began.

Discipline is the ability to live by certain rules or guidelines in order to grow physically, mentally, or spiritually.

FROM GOD'S WORD:

Do not let anyone treat you as if you are unimportant because you are young. Instead, be an example to the believers with your words, your actions, your love, your faith, and your pure life. Until I come, continue to read the Scriptures to the people, strengthen them, and teach them. . . . Continue to do those things; give your life to doing them so your progress may be seen by everyone. Be careful in your life and in your teaching. If you continue to live and teach rightly, you will save both yourself and those who listen to you (1 Timothy 4:12–16).

LET'S TALK ABOUT IT:

1. What were some of the spiritual "disciplines" that The Holy Club thought were important?
2. Why do you think the university officials wanted to stop The Holy Club?
3. What kind of spiritual guidelines or standards do you think might be helpful for you or your family to live by? Why?

BOLDNESS
Rotten Eggs and
Bold Words

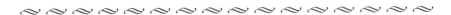

ohn Wesley dodged a rotten egg that flew by his ear and kept on preaching. "God's gift of salvation is for both rich and poor!" Even though Wesley was only five feet and three inches tall, his voice boomed out over the noisy crowd that had gathered in the town square.

"Oh, yeah?" challenged a burly man in workmen's clothes. "Where are *we* gonna get fancy Sunday-go-ta-meetin' clothes? Church is just fer the rich folks."

A chorus of angry voices shouted their agreement. Several more eggs and a rotten tomato flew in Wesley's direction. The little preacher didn't seem upset—but he did think it was ironic.

First, the Church of England wouldn't let him preach in its churches because he preached salvation by faith alone rather than by church traditions and good works. So Wesley decided to preach out in the open to people who didn't usually go to church—in a field, by a city gate, or in the town square. But when he preached to the common people, sometimes they started a riot. What they'd seen of the state religion didn't have much to do with their lives of hunger, misery, and backbreaking work.

"But that's the Good News!" Wesley continued. "Christ died for all people. God loves you—"

"Loves us!" screeched an old woman. "Oh, sure He does! Maybe that's why my old man ran out on me and left me with six young'uns."

Wesley tried to tell the people that God cared about their troubles and would give them strength in their time of need. But by now, the unruly crowd was pushing and shoving, throwing stones and swinging sticks.

Seeing that words wouldn't help, the little preacher jumped off the box he'd been standing on and marched up to the man who seemed to be the ringleader. He took the man's hand and shouted in his ear, "My good man, come with me to my rooms. We can talk there."

Surprised at Wesley's friendly touch, the man suddenly became protective. He kept the crowd away while they went inside the house where Wesley was staying. When the man came out again, he gruffly told the rowdy people that if anyone bothered the preacher anymore, they'd have to answer to him.

Had Wesley threatened the man? No, the traveling preacher asked about the man's family and his worries and explained once again that God's gift of salvation and forgiveness was for him, too. And before Wesley left that English town, he formed one of his "Methodist Societies" to encourage and teach people who were interested in "salvation by faith."

When it was time to move on, John Wesley got on his faithful horse, started in the direction of the next town, then opened a book to read on the way—until he got to the next town and had to face the next wild mob.

Boldness is the confidence to speak out for God, even when others do not want you to.

FROM GOD'S WORD:

Always be ready to answer everyone who asks you to explain about the hope you have, but answer in a gentle way and with respect. Keep a clear conscience so that those who speak evil of your good life in Christ will be made ashamed (1 Peter 3:15b–16).

LET'S TALK ABOUT IT:

1. Why were *both* the rich people *and* the poor people against John Wesley's preaching?
2. How did Wesley win over the wild mob?
3. The verse above tells us to be bold ("always be ready to answer everyone"), but . . . what kind of boldness? Pray together as a family for boldness that talks to people with gentleness and respect.

GENEROSITY
Taming the Money Monster

retend that you are a modern newspaper reporter interviewing John Wesley, the traveling Methodist preacher who lived in the eighteenth century. You want to know what he thinks about a very modern subject . . . MONEY.

YOU: Reverend Wesley, if you were preaching today, what would you tell Christians about money?

JOHN WESLEY: First of all, I would tell them to "GAIN ALL YOU CAN."

YOU: What? I expected you to say that money was the root of all sorts of evil, like greed and stealing and gambling.

JOHN WESLEY: The *love* of money is the root of all evil—not money itself. But sometimes it's hard to know the difference between money and the love of it. That's why I have three principles about money.

YOU: Okay, so the first one is to "gain all you can."

JOHN WESLEY: Yes. But it's important *how* we gain our money. We must not gain money in ways that hurt our bodies—jobs that are unhealthy or prevent us from getting our proper food and rest.

YOU: Like breathing pesticides or being a workaholic, for instance.

JOHN WESLEY: Exactly. Also, we must not make money in ways that hurt our minds and spirits—anything that is sinful or against the laws of God or our country.

YOU: That's right! You used to preach against the slave trade because, even though it was legal, it was against God's commandment to love our neighbor as ourselves.

JOHN WESLEY: Which is another thing. We must gain all we can *without hurting our neighbor*—either our neighbor's body or his soul.

YOU: I see. That rules out a lot of things—like businesses that take advantage of poor people, or making violent movies, or dealing drugs.

JOHN WESLEY: But it leaves a lot of things we *can* do by hard work and common sense.

YOU: But "gain all you can" is only the first principle. What about the second?

JOHN WESLEY: The second is, "SAVE ALL YOU CAN."

YOU: You mean, like in a savings account?

JOHN WESLEY: Not exactly. I mean, don't waste your money on unnecessary things. Plan to have some left over after you've given your family the basic things they need to live.

YOU: But most people think that the reason to "gain all you can" is so you can "spend all you can."

JOHN WESLEY: Ah! But there's a difference for the Christian. The Christian wants to "gain all you can" and "save all you can" so you can "GIVE ALL YOU CAN."

YOU: I knew there was a catch.

JOHN WESLEY: Remember that everything we have already belongs to God. After we take care of the needs of our family, we are encouraged to "do good to all people, especially to those who belong to the family of believers."

YOU: Wow! That really makes sense. Now I understand something I read about you. When you were a young man, you made 30 pounds (English money); you lived on 28 pounds and had 2 pounds to give away. The next year, you doubled your money to 60 pounds, but you still lived on 28 so you had 32 to give away. And when you made 120 pounds a year, you *still* lived on 28 and gave away 92!

JOHN WESLEY (laughing): I call it Kingdom economics!

Generosity in giving to others is simply giving back to God what belongs to Him in the first place.

FROM GOD'S WORD:
He will make you rich in every way so that you can always give freely. And your giving through us will cause many to give thanks to God (2 Corinthians 9:11).

LET'S TALK ABOUT IT:
1. What were John Wesley's three principles about money?
2. How did he apply this in his own life?
3. As a family, brainstorm ways you can "gain all you can, save [not waste] all you can, and give all you can."

List of Character Qualities

BOLDNESS
   "Come Hear a Woman Preach!" (William & Catherine Booth)
   The Night Chicago Burned (Dwight L. Moody)
   Taking New York (Samuel Morris)
   Rotten Eggs and Bold Words (John Wesley)

COMPASSION
   "The Child-Catching Missie Ammal" (Amy Carmichael)
   Blow to the Forehead (Harriet Tubman)

CONFIDENCE
   Not Good Enough (Gladys Aylward)

COURAGE
   The Man With the Axe (Gladys Aylward)
   "Here I Stand!" (Martin Luther)
   The Bully's Challenge (Mary Slessor)

CREATIVITY
   The General's Boxer (William & Catherine Booth)

DEDICATION
   "Doctor Livingstone, I Presume?" (David Livingstone)

DISCIPLINE
   Training for a Young Soldier (William & Catherine Booth)
   The Holy Club (John Wesley)

ENCOURAGEMENT
   Take Heart! (Samuel Morris)

DAVE AND NETA JACKSON are an award-winning husband-and-wife writing team, the authors or coauthors of over a hundred books. They are most well-known for the TRAILBLAZERS, a forty-book series of historical fiction about great Christian heroes for young readers (with sales topping 1.7 million), and Neta's popular *Yada Yada Prayer Group* novels for women.

Dave and Neta bring their love for historical research to the four-volume series of HERO TALES. Each book features fifteen Christian heroes, highlighting important character qualities through forty-five nonfiction stories from their lives.

The Jacksons make their home in the Chicago metropolitan area, where they are active in cross-cultural ministry and enjoy their grandchildren.

Don't Stop Now!

Enjoy More Dramatic Stories From Lives of Christian Heroes With *Hero Tales*, Volumes II, III, and IV!

These *Hero Tales* books are also beautifully illustrated collections of exciting and inspirational readings. Courage, faith, perseverance, mercy, and many more godly characteristics are revealed in the lives of men and women in every era of history. These books will make everyone in the family want to live more fully for Jesus.

Hero Tales: Volume II
Includes: Corrie ten Boom, Florence Nightingale, Jim Elliot, and others!

Hero Tales: Volume III
Includes: Billy Graham, Mother Teresa, Brother Andrew, and others!

Hero Tales: Volume IV
Includes: C.S. Lewis, Joy Ridderhof, Ben Carson, and others!

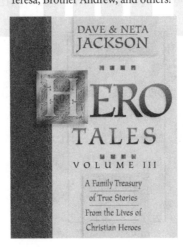

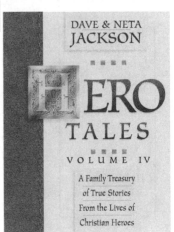